楽々日本料理

JAPANESE COMFORT COOKING

JAPANESE COMFORT COOKING

An Opinionated Guide to Modern, Homey, Classic Japanese Recipes

TADASHI ONO
& HARRIS SALAT

PHOTOGRAPHS BY
JANICE CHUNG

TEN SPEED PRESS
California | New York

ハムカツ
梅水晶
梅酒
魚

メキシカン
料理
生ビール
鍛冶町酒場
Wagyu Yakiniku
神田精肉店
大衆酒場
焼肉
居酒屋
やきとり
Mexican Food
PIZZA
STAND
BAR
生ビール190
黒毛和牛480

CONTENTS

1 MISO SOUP (AND OTHER SOUPS) 味噌汁、汁

2 RICE 米

3 NOODLES 麺

4 SALADS AND VEGETARIAN SOZAI サラダ、惣菜

5 (MORE AMAZING) VEGETABLES 野菜

6 FISH 魚

7 SHELLFiSH 甲殻類

8 EGGS, CHiCKEN, AND DUCK 卵、鶏、鴨

9 BEEF, PORK, AND LAMB 牛、豚、羊

神奈川
大根
1本 180円
神奈川
キャベツ
1コ 330円
静岡産
レタス
1コ 280
三浦市農研
共販
カルラディ
やわらかい
静岡
キャンディキャベツ
1コ 500円
徳島産
里浦大根
ずっしり重く
みずみずしい
普通の大根とはひと味違う
甘みがありみずみずしいのが特徴です
通常の大根と比べると味染み込み
やすいのも特徴です
煮込み料理にもってこいです
1本 300えん
熊本
スティックセニョール

あります♪
お入り下さい!
こども
110番
のいえ
甘酒
(冬期のみ)
350円
おしるこ
五八〇円
みそ田楽
三五〇円
うわさの『勝浦』
タンタンカップ麺
330円

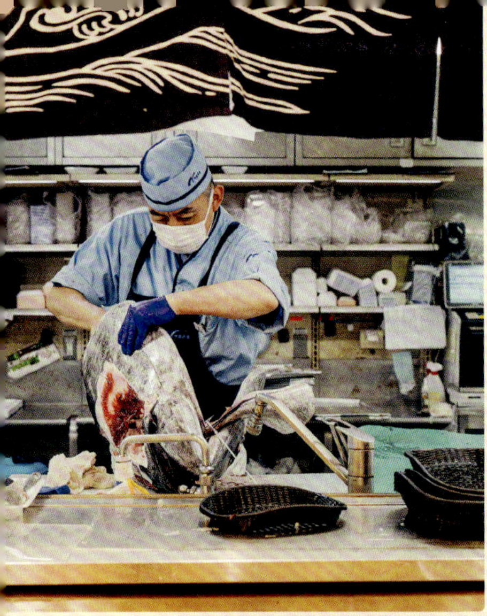

INTRODUCTION

Fifteen years ago we wrote a book called *Japanese Soul Cooking,* which told the stories of Japanese dishes that originated in the last decades of the nineteenth century, soon after the Emperor sank his molars into a hearty hunk of beef—the first time the first son of the Rising Sun did that in a thousand years. (That bite was a *big* deal.) We helped home cooks across the world unlock a delicious and beloved culinary world.

We won accolades, praise, and spots on "best cookbook" lists. . . . But much more important, you—our dear readers—spread the love far and wide through word of mouth (and wonderful Amazon reviews) and people are still discovering the book today. For that, we are humbled and grateful.

In the more than a decade since publishing the book, the two of us did a bunch of stuff, including partnering in the hectic New York City restaurant business. But, hey, through it all, we're still friends! Now we're back to scratch an unrequited cooking itch, something we've been talking about for years, something we want, no, *need* to share with readers. We're talking about Japanese comfort food.

What is Japanese comfort food? It's a crazy quilt blend of traditional *washoku* classics and modern, inventive cooking. It's miso soup, soba noodles, cured fish, and vegetables steeped in fragrant umami seasonings. It's also Japanese-style sandwiches, salads, steak, *wagyu* burgers, *gobo* fries, roasted vegetables, and baked chicken. It's cooking that doesn't live under museum glass, never to be touched or altered. It's both deeply of the culture and boldly influenced by American, Chinese, Korean, and European chow flashing on TikTok, Instagram, and Line (the Japanese super app). It's the grub that gets pumped out of home kitchens and neighborhood joints alike, and what people in Japan actually eat every day. Listen up, people: Japanese comfort announces itself loud and proud!

And the best part?

This cooking is *raku-raku,* Japanese lingo for "easy peasy" or "piece of cake." These are dishes anyone can knock out, totally accessible to cooks of all culinary stripes—with our help, of course. In the pages that follow, we'll show you how, step by step, through straightforward recipes, instructional photos, and demystified ingredients. (Ingredients, by the way, that are a "buy now" button-click away from any cook, coast to coast.) And we'll head to Japan to drill down to culinary bedrock and tell you the fascinating and surprising stories behind dishes, ingredients, techniques, and more.

You're in good hands here. Tadashi is a storied Japanese chef who grew up with this chow in Tokyo's version of the Boogie Down Bronx and originally landed in California to surf (he still surfs). His culinary Yellow Brick Road led from Japanese cooking to acclaimed French fine dining until, ultimately, he heard the siren call of his roots and helmed some of the hippest Japanese restaurants in New York. Harris is a journalist and cook who fell in love with this fare while traveling to Japan and writing about the food culture there; to get tactile with it, he interned in Tadashi's restaurant kitchen and others in Tokyo and Kyoto. We met a couple of decades ago and kicked off a conversation about Japanese cooking—over too many beers and bottles of sake and many fantastic meals—that continues to this day.

HOW TO COOK THIS BOOK

This book is an opinionated guide. We have a point of view. And the first particular point of our view is, this cooking is absolutely achievable. As you'll see in the recipes, the cooking is simple, but it's a simplicity that has to be learned (hat tip to author and journalist Bill Buford!).

Harris has something he likes to call "the refrigerator test." Whenever he visits a home in Japan, his favorite part is watching everyday cooks magically conjure a sublime meal from whatever they find in the fridge—with the aid of key seasonings like dashi, soy sauce, mirin, sake, and miso. We want to help you summon this same wizardry. You'll see our recipes include tons of options for alternative ingredients, flavors, and accents. We want you to try stuff, have fun, and get into the Japanese cooking groove.

A few things to keep in mind:

The Tadashi way is cooking with intention. His recipes are straightforward, but they humbly ask you to pay attention, taste, and practice. For some of you, this is a brand-new cuisine. Read the recipes top to bottom before you start. Prep ingredients before you cook. The more dishes you try, the more you'll develop a feel for Japanese flavors and techniques, and how to use them. In Chinese, *kung fu* means a discipline you practice your whole life but never fully master. The Japanese word for that is *dō*. It's a beautiful sensibility. Japanese cooking is a *dō*. Embrace it. Enjoy it. Our wish is that your Japanese culinary adventure evolves from following our recipes to understanding the principles they teach—and ultimately acing your own refrigerator test.

Tadashi likes to say that traditional food producers do most of the work in Japanese cuisine. What he means is that the process of fermenting soy sauce, mirin, sake, and miso unlocks so much glorious flavor, depth, and umami that you can create a delicious dish without too much cooking effort. That's a huge difference from Western cuisine. In Japanese cooking you're not braising something for hours to tease out flavor; the traditional seasonings do that heavy flavor lifting for you. So the cooking here is fast, and most of the dishes in this book qualify for your weeknight dinner rotation. We hope you add them to the lineup.

Taste your food as you cook. Oh, we said that already, but it bears repeating. Figure out what *you* like. This cooking is incredibly flexible. Not salty enough? Add a dab more soy sauce! Like it spicier? Tobanjan is your friend. Allergic to sesame? Sub sesame oil with avocado oil and omit the sesame seeds. (You'll lose a layer of flavor, but there's usually so much else going on that it's fine.) No gluten? No problem. You can find terrific gluten-free soy sauce and noodles. Plant-based diet? Pull up a stool. We love veggies and include two chapters worth of fantastic all-vegetarian recipes.

Finally, let's talk about sugar. You'll see recipes where we add sugar to the dishes. If you're not familiar with Japanese cuisine, this can seem odd. But rest easy. Japanese cooking is centered on balance rather than impact. What does that mean? Western cooking is about layering spice, fat, and heat to deliver a hardy flavor wallop. In Japanese cooking, you're looking for harmony. That's where sugar and the sweetness in mirin, which you'll learn about shortly, come in. Their job is to level the savoriness of soy sauce and miso, so the natural flavors of the underlying ingredients shine through.

HOW TO EAT THIS BOOK

Not literally, we hope! What we mean is: how to eat the Japanese way.

First, forget the appetizer-to-main-course orthodoxy, okay? Japanese meals revolve around a procession of dishes, built on a traditional framework known as *ichiju sansai*, or "one soup, three dishes." The idea here is simple: a bowl of soup, usually miso soup, steamed rice, and three or so small dishes featuring veggies, meat, fish, or tofu. And no guilt trips. If you want to cook, say, karaage, the Japanese version of fried chicken (basically the best fried chicken on planet Earth), you're not sizzling a bucketful of drumsticks—you're preparing and enjoying a few rich pieces of chicken, paired with a variety of other tasty stuff. The sum of which is an incredibly satisfying meal.

In fact, building a Japanese meal traditionally revolves around the power of "five": five flavors (*gomi*)—sweet, salty, sour, bitter, and umami; five colors (*goshiki*)—white, yellow, red, green, and black; five cooking methods (*goho*)—raw, simmered, steamed, grilled, and fried; and five senses (*gokan*)—sight, sound, smell, touch, and taste. Mix and match these fives, and you're eating a healthy, delicious, delightful meal by definition—without having to think about it! Ingenious!

This all sounds great, but you might be thinking: How in the hades am I supposed to cook a bunch of dishes at 6 p.m. on a Thursday after a long day of work with hungry, screaming significant others/kids/friends itching to chow down?

Hold on. Remember what we said about fast and easy? This is what Japanese cooking is all about. Most of the recipes here you can whip up faster than zapping a frozen lasagna in the microwave. And if you listen to Tadashi, you'll be prepping *sozai* side dishes you cook once and enjoy over a few meals (see Chapter 4), freezing cooked rice, and freezing dashi for a quick soup. We've got you covered. And when you do have time or are cooking with loved ones or friends, try more involved recipes (like Yaki Sabazushi, page 150).

Finally, Japanese food is not just about all that delicious cooking. It's also a feast for the eyes, and soul. Have fun with your presentation. Don't use only white plates. Mix and match tableware. Try different colors, shapes, and textures—get creative and playful with your meal! Even for a quick dinner. This is part of the joy of Japanese cuisine.

(In fact, the bulk of the lovely tableware we photograph in this book are Tadashi's and Harris's personal Japanese wares that they cherish deeply, including dishes that Tadashi, who's also an accomplished potter, made himself.)

Okay, this is all just the tip of the bamboo shoot to get you started. We'll be unpacking much, much more Japanese comfort cooking know-how, insights, and fun facts in the pages and recipes that follow. Buckle up!

(And hey, we'd love to see what you cook. Send us pictures! And also any questions or comments at hello@japanesecomfortcooking.com or DM @japanesecomfortcooking on Instagram.)

つくば商事
徒歩
1分
賃貸
管理
売買
開発
SINCE 1967
つくば商事 検索
不動産
株式会社 つくば商事
TEL
3268-0201

AOKI
大井町駅前
りんかい線
atré 2

JAPANESE INGREDIENTS TO KNOW

FERMENTED SEASONINGS

Stock your kitchen with these key fermented seasonings:

Japanese Soy Sauce

Japanese soy sauce is its own thing and differs from Chinese and other regional varieties. Called *shoyu* in Japanese, it has a complex, nuanced flavor with a hint of sweetness. Look for shoyu with these four ingredients, and no other junk: water, soybeans, wheat, and salt. (If you're wheat-sensitive, fear not—Kikkoman produces a solid gluten-free shoyu that you can easily find online.) There are three main styles of shoyu to know about, and we use them all in this cookbook.

Koikuchi is the all-purpose shoyu that's the workhorse of Japanese cooking. Any Japanese soy sauce with no other descriptors is koikuchi. And if you want to kick your koikuchi game up a notch, look for a variety called *marudaizu shoyu*. This soy sauce is brewed from whole soybeans and is fermented and aged longer than standard soy sauce, yielding a deeper, subtler flavor and more complex umami. But don't sweat it if you can't find marudaizu . . . good ol' standard shoyu is perfectly fine!

Usukuchi is shoyu that hails from the Kyoto region and is often confusingly described in English as "light" soy sauce. While "light" here usually means fewer calories or less sodium, or something like that, usukuchi is called "light" because it's lighter in *color*. In fact, it has *more* salt than all-purpose koikuchi. That said, we use usukuchi in more delicate dishes, thanks to its lighter color and less dominant soy-saucy flavor.

Tamari shoyu dates back to the seventh century, when soy fermentation techniques arrived in Japan from China. Brewed from soybeans, water, and salt, it's traditionally made from the liquid that accumulates during miso fermentation. Tamari is wonderful but sometimes thought of in the United States as "better" than regular shoyu. It's not better; it's different (just like Dijon and yellow are both mustards, but different). Its powerful, complex flavor works great in dipping sauces (like those served with sashimi) and marinades, but you don't want to wholesale substitute all-purpose shoyu with it. Too intense.

Mirin

Mirin is another key fermented seasoning that adds delicate sweetness, body, and umami to dishes. Originally enjoyed as a sweet alcoholic beverage, traditional mirin—which is brewed from mochi rice (sticky rice), koji (see page 22), and shochu (spirit)—is expensive and not easy to find. So we rely on the industrially produced version. Look for mirin with the fewest ingredients. And cooking with mirin quickly evaporates the alcohol, so that's not an issue. (In some dishes we purposely cook off the mirin's alcohol first.)

Sake

Sake is Japan's national alcoholic beverage, brewed from water and fermented rice, with a two-thousand-year history (for more on sake, see page 146). It also plays an integral role in Japanese cooking, adding depth, complexity, body, and umami flavor to foods, while complementing shoyu and mirin. An indispensable seasoning! And one that's incredibly versatile and used to enhance so many dishes. Now, what to buy: Good-quality drinking sake is too precious to cook with, and so-called cooking sake available in Asian markets is ultra-processed and loaded with junk ingredients like corn syrup. Avoid it! We like to use a basic, California-made sake like Gekkeikan—it is the real thing, inexpensive, and can sit in the fridge for a month.

Miso

Miso is deep. A fundamental ingredient in Japanese cooking for more than 1,300 years, it's a paste made by fermenting soybeans, salt, and rice or sometimes barley. (There's also a miso fermented from just soybeans and salt called *hatcho,* see page 98.) What's so cool about miso is that it evolved in ancient times as a way for people to consume soybeans, which are packed with protein but hard to digest. Fermentation is essentially pre-digesting them—so their protein and nutrients are easier to absorb. And better yet, miso is a probiotic food with live active cultures, so it's good for you in so many ways! But of course, health benefits aren't the only reason miso is so important in Japanese cooking. This paste adds its magical, earthy-savory-umami-powered flavor to everything from soup to fish to meat to vegetables. There's nothing else quite like it. Japan produces more than a thousand misos, which, like wine, express their own unique flavor profiles, ingredients, regional traditions, and terroir.

Miso can be fermented for as little as a few weeks or for two to three years—or more. *Shiro,* or savory white miso, is fermented for about a year, while *aka,* or red miso, bubbles away in cedar barrels, which bestow its trademark ruddy hue, for two to three years. So, which miso to use? General rule of thumb: Use lighter miso for preparing veggies, fish, or chicken, and darker, longer-fermented miso for cooking meat. There are lots of exceptions. Most important, use what *you* enjoy.

Look for miso with just two or three ingredients: soybeans and salt; soybeans, salt, and rice; or soybeans, salt, and barley. A few misos we love:

- *Saikyo,* the signature miso of Kyoto is lightly fermented with a mellow sweetness.
- *Sendai,* a rich, coarse aka miso from Japan's far northern snow country.
- *Shinshu,* between shiro and aka, hailing from the Japanese Alps (the country's biggest miso-producing region).
- *Mugi,* a barley-based staple of Japan's deep south, the island of Kyushu.

There are also American producers who make great miso, so give those a try, too. Combine different misos to create your own bespoke *awase* (mixed) miso. As with wine, try various kinds and figure out what you like.

みなみぐら

THE MIRACLE OF KOJI

Let's talk briefly about Japan's "national mold." Come again? Koji mold, or for all you bio majors out there, *Aspergillus oryzae*, is the foundational building block of all traditional seasonings we introduce here, from miso to soy sauce to mirin to sake. No mold, no Japanese food. Seriously. Why? Because koji produces enzymes that break down the complex molecules in soybeans, rice, and other staples to unlock aroma, rich flavor, and the cuisine's signature deep umami taste. And beyond its gustatory benefits, koji acts as a natural preservative, inhibiting the growth of harmful bacteria that helps these seasonings last longer. One rockin' mold! Koji's Japanese culinary roots stretch back some two thousand years. In 2006, the Brewing Society of Japan honored that legacy by anointing it with the title of *kokkin*, or National Fungus.

MORE KEY INGREDIENTS

Rice Vinegar

While conventional, mass-produced white vinegar is fermented from corn, Japanese rice vinegar is traditionally slow-brewed from rice through a two-stage fermentation process that can take several months. Thanks to this leisurely pace, it develops a complex and mellower flavor than its bland mass-produced cousin, with a lower acidity and a subtle sweetness, adding brightness and deliciousness that never overpowers other ingredients. Store rice vinegar in a cool, dark place (not the fridge); its flavors will deepen over time.

Tobanjan

Tobanjan is a Japanese version of the Sichuanese staple known as *doubanjiang* in Mandarin. Both are fiery pastes produced from fermented broad beans and chile peppers. The Japanese version is not as head-explodingly hot and has a smoother consistency. It's salty, savory, and a little bit funky, which is why we love it. Beyond the uses in this book, try it in other dishes if you want to add a tasty kick (as we do with Japanese fried rice on page 74). One note: A little bit of this stuff goes a long way.

Neri Goma

Literally "kneaded sesame," this Japanese sesame paste is used in a bunch of recipes. Available in white or black, the seeds are roasted longer than those used for the better-known tahini, giving it a more intense, nuttier flavor. You can find it in Japanese and (maybe) Asian markets, or online. In a pinch, substitute with tahini.

Arajio

Japan lacks natural salt deposits so all domestically produced salt comes from the sea. Arajio is a pure, natural sea salt that's sun dried using traditional methods. It's sold either dry or wet. The wet variety is lovely; there's still a hint of brine that adds an incredibly flavorful minerality to its bracing saltiness. You can find it in Japanese markets. Squeeze the package, the salt will feel damp. (Also, keep in mind that while arajio is wonderful, good ol' reliable kosher salt works perfectly for all our recipes, so don't sweat the salt!)

JAPANESE ACCENTS

Use these accents to give dishes an extra burst of flavor. Besides the ingredients we discuss next, Japanese cooking relies on *shibori* scallions (see page 41); *hari shoga* (needle-cut ginger, see page 112); finely sliced or chopped aromatic shiso leaves (a relative of the mint family, which comes in red or green); and that workhorse of accents, white or black toasted sesame seeds.

Yuzu Kosho

We're puzzled that yuzu kosho isn't as much of a household name as sriracha. It's such a super flavorful and versatile condiment, made from just three ingredients fermented together: yuzu, chile peppers, and salt. This particular alchemy delivers an incredibly aromatic, citrusy, mouthwatering paste lavished with bracing heat. So amazing! There are two kinds: green, made with green yuzu peel and green chile peppers, which has a sharper flavor and is hotter; and red, made with ripened yellow yuzu peel and red chile peppers, which is more fragrant and citrusy. Which to use? All of the above! We swoon over both and call for them early and often in our recipes. Beyond the recipes, add a dab to liven up your next bowl of miso soup, ramen, or other soupy noodles; give a boost to simple salt-grilled fish, chicken, or meat; or add zing to a quick marinade (see page 153). Rule of thumb: red for fish or chicken, green for meat. But as with miso, these aren't laws etched in stone tablets—follow your bliss, always!

Karashi

This traditional mustard is made from only crushed brown mustard seeds and water, with no vinegar or other ingredients usually found in mustards. So it's much more potent, intense, and sinus-clearing—a dab is enough to liven a dish! It comes in powder form (mix it with water) or as a premade paste.

Wasabi

If you buy a tube of "wasabi," chances are it's made from horseradish, mustard, and food coloring. That ain't wasabi. The real thing is a rhizome native to Japan that grows along cold mountain streams and takes one to one-and-a-half years to mature. The real thing is bright green when grated and has a beautiful, complex flavor that's sharp and pungent but not nearly as fiery as the fake stuff. Wasabi has been integral to Japanese cuisine since ancient times, prized for its ability to elevate ingredients like raw fish and for its natural antibacterial properties. The good news is that real wasabi is readily available in Asian markets (like H-Mart) both as a fresh rhizome and in the frozen section. Give it a try.

Shichimi Togarashi

Literally "seven-flavor chili pepper," this versatile seasoning was invented in the early 1600s at a shop in Tokyo called Yagenbori that's still in business today. A powdery blend of ground red chile pepper, sansho, roasted orange peel, ground ginger, and other aromatics, shichimi togarashi can be sprinkled as a finishing touch to add subtle heat, flavor, and fragrance to almost any dish. (Don't confuse it with ichimi togarashi, which is pure red chile pepper.)

Sansho

Ground from the berries of the Japanese prickly ash tree, sansho has a history stretching back thousands of years as both a spice and a medicinal ingredient. Intensely aromatic, it adds tangy, citrusy notes as well as subtle heat and a slight numbing effect (it's a relative of the Sichuan peppercorn, but much less potent). It's a super versatile natural flavor enhancer that stimulates your taste buds and lavishes flavor and fragrance on a wide range of dishes.

築地
正本

JAPANESE KITCHEN EQUIPMENT TO KNOW

We're not big on the million-gadgets-in-the-kitchen approach to cooking. Here are the essential tools we rely on:

Japanese Kitchen Knife

Back in the day, a samurai's sword was considered a projection of his warrior soul—his most precious possession. This sensibility was adopted by Japanese cooks over time, and the craftsmanship that defined the *katana,* or sword, inspired a bevy of traditional kitchen knives: specialized blades designed for slicing everything from tuna to tomatoes. With the exception of one specialized knife (maybe, see Honesuki below), you don't need a half-dozen traditional Japanese blades in your home kitchen. What we recommend are two types of *gyuto.* Originally designed for cutting meat (*gyu* means "beef"), the gyuto resembles a Western chef's knife in shape and has evolved into an all-purpose kitchen knife. By "two versions," we mean an 8- to 11-inch primary blade (we like 'em bigger!) and a 4- to 5-inch petty knife for small jobs. That's it.

So if a gyuto approximates a Wüsthof, what's the difference? Japanese knives feature lighter, thinner blades forged from harder steel than their Western counterparts, so you can cut with greater precision, and the blade doesn't dull as quickly. (But hard steel is brittle, so don't drop your knife!) Are they expensive? Yes. Are they worth it? Hell yes. Look, you don't need a butcher block of knives. If you show your Japanese knives loving care, they'll last for decades. (Both of us have sliced with our beloved Japanese blades for years and years and years—and counting.)

For most cutting jobs, grasp your Japanese knife by pinching the top of the blade with your thumb and index finger for better control (wrap the rest of your fingers around the handle). Slice *through* ingredients by sliding the blade forward, rather than crushing down on them, to produce clean, beautiful cuts. (Check out a YouTube video on Japanese cutting techniques to see what we mean.) Keep your knife sharp, which is actually safer in the kitchen because your knife will glide through foods with less resistance. (Here's another YouTube homework assignment—look up sharpening techniques for Japanese knives.) Store your knife in a sheath to protect the blade. And always use a good-quality *manaita,* or cutting board, which will extend the life of your knife. Finally, note that Japanese knives are not forged with bolsters, the thick part of a Western blade where the metal meets the handle to help protect your hand. Why does this matter? Because if you're used to Western knives and new to the Japanese variety, you can cut the crap out of yourself with the heel of the blade if you're not careful—as Harris can attest from his early days using these knives. But with a little practice, your Japanese blade will become an extension of your hand, and dare we say, your spirit.

Honesuki

Okay, we said we'd offer one possible exception to the two-knife rule: the *honesuki.* Literally "bone knife," the honesuki is a thick, heavy knife with a small, rigid 4- to 6-inch blade that tapers to a fine point. Precision-designed for breaking down and deboning poultry, its unique construction helps you "feel" where joints are when you're, say, working a chicken leg. If you're going to splurge on an extra knife, consider the honesuki.

Otama

If a soup spoon and a Western-style ladle had a love child, it would look like an *otama*. This traditional Japanese ladle has a long handle and a wide, shallow bowl that's almost like a giant spoon, but deeper. Its unique design gives you more precise control than Western versions, making it easier to skim off scum from stocks, serve soup without dripping, and even quickly sip your cooking liquid (always taste as you cook!). Otama come in different sizes, from the standard kitchen version that holds about ½ cup of liquid to smaller ones.

Saibashi

Chopsticks are super precise dining instruments, allowing you to grab even a single grain of rice (we dare you to try that with a fork!). *Saibashi* are an extension of this exactitude, but for the kitchen. Around 13 inches long, usually made from wood or bamboo, which resist heat, these oversize kitchen chopsticks will keep your hands safely out of range of steam, splattering oil, and high temps while you cook. They're indispensable for stirring, mixing, and turning ingredients in a skillet or in hot broth. You'll need to practice a bit to get comfortable using them, but we love their finesse and versatility—which put standard-issue tongs to shame.

Suribachi and Surikogi

This is a traditional Japanese mortar and pestle that comes in a wide range of sizes, from tiny to giant. The bowl is ceramic and glazed on the outside, while the pestle is wood—the most prized versions are made from the wood of the sansho tree (see page 29). The interior of the bowl features concentric grooves called *kushi-no-me,* unlike the smooth interior of Western-style mortars. And that's the suribachi's secret. The grooves let you gently grind sesame seeds and other ingredients without bruising them, and they also help keep ingredients contained while grinding so stuff isn't flying all over the place. The wooden surikogi, meanwhile, works harmoniously with the suribachi and doesn't damage the grooves while grinding. We love using a suribachi and surikoge for all tasks that call for a mortar and pestle, Japanese cooking or not. Place your suribachi on a kitchen towel when you work to help hold it in place.

Oroshigane

This Japanese grater is traditionally handmade from tin-coated copper plates but is now available in more affordable plastic, ceramic, and other metals. Instead of tiny holes through which grated material falls, it features raised teeth that grate finer than Western versions. And that's the beauty of this tool. You typically grate ingredients in a circular motion—crushing ginger, for example—to extract more flavor and juice from its fibers than you could with a Microplane. And when grating ingredients like daikon or *yamaimo* (mountain yam), the oroshigane produces a smooth puree instead of shredded pieces. (There's even a specialized oroshigane made from spiky sharkskin just for grating wasabi that produces the same result.) Processed ingredients stay on top of the oroshigane, so you can slide them into whatever you're cooking.

SURIBACHI
AND SURIKOGE
HONESUKI
GYUTO
OROSHIGANE
SHAMOJI
OTAMA
FISH SPATULA

鳥料理
ひな鳥
やきとり
鳥
ORO
SAPPORO
鳥
ま
す
エビス樽生ビール
尾花沢
小玉西瓜
ぼけしらずネギ

1

MISO SOUP

味噌汁、汁

[AND OTHER SOUPS]

A staple for more than 1,300 years, miso soup is a big deal in Japanese cooking. Samurai sported something called *imogara nawa,* a belt knotted from dried taro stems that had been simmered in miso. Pop that stem into a bowl of boiling water, and you've got the original cup-a-soup. We found research saying that even now, in modern times, three quarters of Japanese people sip a bowl of miso soup every single day.

Miso soup is the foundation of the traditional eating structure called *ichiju sansai,* or "one soup, three dishes." And for good reason. Miso soup perks you up like coffee—from its super healthy nutrients, not caffeine. Researchers have found it can lower blood pressure and risk of certain cancers; it can have anti-aging, anti-diabetic, and anti-inflammatory effects; and its live bacteria culture serves as a powerful probiotic. So much goodness going on!

But of course, there's another reason miso soup is so elemental to Japanese cooking: It's incredibly delicious. And flexible. And easy to prepare.

A few things to keep in mind: Miso soup starts with cooking ingredients in dashi. *Dashi* means, simply, "stock." Classic dashi is conjured from kombu and dried, shaved bonito fish. Other versions include an all-vegetarian one teased from dried shiitake mushrooms. We share recipes for both here. What's so interesting about dashi is that it developed in response to a ban on eating meat by one Emperor Tenmu for religious reasons, a prohibition that lasted for more than a thousand years. So relying on meat and bones to power a stock was out. Instead, cooks evolved a tasty workaround in dashi, which leans on mouthwatering umami flavors, way before anyone knew what umami was (see Umami Power!, opposite). Chalk one up for the human spirit!

Whatever ingredients you use for miso soup, simmer them until just cooked through so they retain their natural flavor and infuse the dashi with more depth. Most miso soups feature just two or three main ingredients—remember, you're not cooking gumbo. Choose ingredients that offer complementary or contrasting textures, colors, or flavors, and cut everything into bite-size pieces you can grab with chopsticks. The idea is to be playful and have fun.

Once ingredients are set, you're ready to add miso (see page 20). The general ratio is ¼ cup miso for 4 cups dashi. Miso tastes very salty, but this ratio adds just enough of the fermented paste to flavor the soup but not overwhelm it. We share two options to dissolve miso in your soup. Either way, as soon as the miso is dissolved, briefly (and gently) simmer on low heat just to blend the flavors, then serve immediately. Miso is a live culture like yogurt so you don't want to boil it.

Garnish your soup with shibori scallions (see page 41), shichimi togarashi, sesame seeds, grated ginger, or sansho, and soup's on!

In the pages that follow we'll share some of our favorite miso soup recipes for every season. We also add some other classic Japanese soups that we know you'll love, too. Like we said, miso soup is very flexible. Want more heft? Swirl in beaten eggs along with the miso, crack an egg into a soup to poach it, add cooked somen noodles (see page 80), or mix in cooked rice (this combination is referred to, charmingly, as *inu meshi*—dog food). Mix and match different kinds of miso (called *awase* miso) to create bespoke flavors. Experiment with ingredients and come up with your own favorite soups. In addition to the recipes, we list a bunch of combinations here. Enjoy!

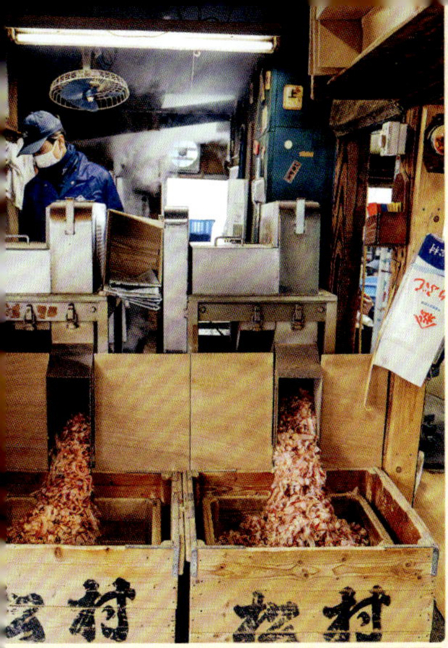

UMAMI POWER!

Okay, pop quiz: What do a chunk of Parmesan, a dry-aged porterhouse, and a rich marinara sauce have in common? Answer: In each of these foods, aging, fermentation, or cooking breaks down proteins into their building blocks—amino acids and other compounds. One of those amino acids, glutamate, triggers an intensely savory, mouthwatering, mouth-filling, lingering sensation on the tongue. That, friends, is umami.

Now recognized as the fifth basic taste alongside sweet, sour, salty, and bitter, umami has long starred as the cornerstone taste of Japanese cuisine. Why are key fermented seasonings like soy sauce, mirin, sake, and miso so incredibly flavorful? Umami. Why does dashi infuse ingredients with so much deliciousness? Yep, you guessed right.

What's amazing about Japanese cooking is that these seasonings and dashi instantly deliver a whammy of umami to dishes without a ton of complicated preparation. As Tadashi likes to say, traditional Japanese food producers do most of the cooking work for you. Thank you, traditional food producers!

Dashi itself is truly remarkable. As we mentioned, it evolved as an alternative to extracting stock from animal bones, prompted by Japan's thousand-year ban on meat eating. Classic dashi is teased from kombu and katsuobushi. Kombu is a type of edible kelp that grows naturally in the icy waters off Hokkaido island, in Japan's far north, and comes in several varieties. Incredibly, when dried to naturally preserve it, kombu packs the highest natural concentration of glutamate of any food on the planet.

Katsuobushi is known here as "dried, shaved bonito" (*katsuo* is actually Japanese for skipjack tuna)—but that's not the whole story. Twice a year, huge schools of katsuo surge along the Pacific coast of Japan. How did people preserve this mass of fish in the days before refrigeration? About four hundred years ago a process evolved, still used to this day, to naturally preserve katsuo by gutting, boning, cooking, hardwood-smoking, sun-drying, and fermenting (by applying mold). The result: rock-hard loins you could hammer nails with. These loins were then shaved to produce katsuobushi (literally "shaved katsuo"). Now, remember when we said aging + fermenting + cooking equals . . . umami? Yes! Congratulations, you just made Umami Honor Roll! Indeed, katsuobushi is naturally teeming with umami, this time thanks to an umami compound called inosinic acid.

Now here's the payoff: When you gently heat and infuse kombu in water, then steep katsuobushi in that liquid like tea to make dashi, the umami equation is something like 2 + 2 = 50. The synergy between the umami compounds creates the incredibly rich, savory flavor that makes dashi so magical. But there's more—remember the hardwood-smoking? That step infuses dashi with an intoxicating fragrance—as if you're actually *inhaling* umami.

Finally, for all you all-vegetarian peeps out there—fear not. You can create a similar effect by making dashi with dried shiitake mushrooms and kombu. Dried shiitake is loaded with an umami compound called guanylate. When combined with the glutamate in kombu, the synergistic effect greatly amplifies umami deliciousness in shiitake dashi, just like with its katsuobushi cousin.

ALL-PURPOSE DASHI

万能だし

Dashi is essential to Japanese cuisine, a simple yet profoundly flavorful and versatile stock that forms the foundation of this cooking. There are a number of different dashi and endless ways to prepare them. Dashi coaxed from kombu and katsuobushi (dried, shaved bonito) is the fundamental variety, a magical liquid that infuses dishes with intense, umami-powered flavors and a deep, smoky fragrance (the bonito is in fact smoked). Here we share Tadashi's all-purpose version, which yields consistent, easy-to-achieve results. When you prepare the stock, don't toss the used kombu and bonito—they're perfect for tsukudani, a savory-sweet rice topping (see page 71). Finally, if you want to cut a dashi corner, you can find instant dashi packs, which look like teabags of various sizes, or dashi powder. Just make sure the ingredients are all-natural. You'll save time with these, but ain't nothing like the real thing, baby (as the song goes).

MAKES ABOUT 6 CUPS

8 cups plus 2 tablespoons water

2 (6-inch) pieces kombu

1½ ounces dried, shaved bonito (about 3 packed cups)

In a large stockpot, combine 8 cups of the water and the kombu. Steep for 30 minutes to begin to extract the kombu's flavor.

Bring the mixture to a boil over medium heat. As soon as the water starts to boil, remove the kombu. Add the remaining 2 tablespoons water to lower the temperature slightly and prevent the dashi from becoming cloudy.

Add the bonito and stir it once to combine. As soon as the liquid returns to a boil, decrease the heat to low and simmer for 5 minutes. Use a spoon to remove any scum that appears on the surface (it can affect the flavor and clarity of the dashi).

Turn off the heat and let the liquid steep for 15 minutes. Strain through a fine-mesh sieve or a colander lined with cheesecloth. Don't squeeze the bonito flakes, as this can introduce bitter flavors.

Use the dashi immediately, refrigerate for up to 1 week, or freeze for up to 3 months.

P.S. Pour leftover dashi into ice trays to make easy-to-use "dashi cubes" for quick soups or for recipes that call for dashi. This works great for both All-Purpose Dashi and Shiitake Dashi.

SHIBORI SCALLIONS

絞り葱

We rely on this super useful method for garnishing miso soup and other dishes. So what's the big diff between "regular" sliced scallions and *shibori* scallions? When you prepare scallions *shibori,* which means "wrung out," you're squeezing out the sliminess, so just an intense and satisfying green-oniony flavor remains. Bonus: Shibori scallions last longer in the fridge than regular sliced scallions.

MAKES ABOUT ½ CUP

1 bunch scallions

Fill a medium bowl with cold water. Trim the scallions and slice them crosswise as thinly as possible. Plunge the sliced scallions in the cold water and let them soak for about 5 minutes to crisp up.

Squeeze out the scallions in batches: With a slotted spoon or small fine-mesh sieve, scoop out a mound of scallions and place them on a paper towel. Wrap the scallions in the paper towel and, over a sink, squeeze them firmly to remove any liquid and slime. Place the squeezed onions in a sealable jar and repeat the process with the remaining scallions. Shibori scallions will last in the refrigerator for about a week.

SHIITAKE DASHI
椎茸だし

Shiitake dashi is the classic all-vegetarian stock. Use it for vegetarian dishes or as a plant-based alternative to the kombu and bonito-based version in any recipe (especially for the soups that follow). To us, this dashi runs neck and neck with the bonito version in the deliciousness category. The key is the dried shiitake: the drying process concentrates the mushroom's umami and intensifies its flavor. When you steep dried shiitake along with kombu, all of that goodness is released and ready to use. If you can find high-quality *donko* dried shiitake, grab 'em; their thick caps infuse the dashi with even more intense mushroomy flavor. Also, we encourage you to add vegetable scraps—like carrot or asparagus peels, or cabbage or fennel cores—to your shiitake dashi to conjure even more interesting flavor profiles—go crazy and create your own custom varieties!

MAKES ABOUT 6 CUPS

8 cups water

2 (6-inch) pieces kombu

2 ounces dried shiitake mushrooms (10 to 20 pieces, depending on size)

1 cup assorted vegetable scraps, such as carrot peels, asparagus peels, daikon peels, or cabbage cores (optional)

In a large stockpot, combine the water, kombu, and shiitake. Steep for 3 hours or, preferably, overnight.

Place the stockpot over medium heat and bring it to a boil. As soon as the water starts to boil, remove the kombu. If you're using vegetable scraps, add them now. Reduce the heat and simmer uncovered for 30 minutes. Skim off any scum that appears on the surface, as it can affect the flavor.

Turn off the heat and let the liquid steep for 15 minutes. Strain through a fine-mesh sieve or a colander lined with cheesecloth. Reserve the rehydrated shiitake for use in other recipes.

Use the dashi immediately, refrigerate for up to 1 week, or freeze for up to 3 months.

CHILLED HEIRLOOM TOMATO AND SILKEN TOFU MISO SOUP

トマトと豆腐の冷製味噌汁

Your mission here is to find the tastiest vine-ripened tomatoes possible. Beefsteak, heirloom, even little cherries work, as long as they're ripe and flavorful. Silken tofu, called *kinugoshi* in Japanese, is soft tofu with a delicate, fresh soybean flavor. Domestic versions are perfectly good, but if you can find imported silken tofu from Japan (often available at Japanese and Korean markets), we urge you to try it; the taste is even more sublime. Adding the tomato at the very end of cooking infuses the soup with lovely flavor, creating a refreshing summer dish.

SERVES 4

4 cups dashi (page 40)

¼ cup shiro miso (see page 20)

1 large vine-ripened beefsteak or other tomato (about ½ pound), cut into bite-size pieces

1 container silken tofu (about 12 ounces), drained

¼ cup Shibori Scallions (page 41)

In a medium saucepan, bring the dashi to a boil over medium heat.

To dissolve the miso, you have two choices: If you have a strainer that fits inside your saucepan, add the miso to the strainer and dunk it into the broth. Dissolve the miso with a spoon, pressing against the sides of the strainer. Or add the miso to a small bowl and pour in about ½ cup of the broth. Whisk to dissolve, then add the mixture to the broth, stirring gently to combine. Reduce the heat to low.

Now add the tomatoes. Simmer for another 30 seconds to blend the flavors and harmonize the ingredients, but do not let the soup boil. Remove from the heat.

Allow the miso-tomato broth to cool to room temperature, then transfer it to a sealable container. Refrigerate the broth until chilled, at least 4 hours or overnight.

When you're ready to serve, scoop about ¼ cup tofu into each bowl with a spoon. Pour the chilled broth over the tofu, garnish with the scallions, and serve.

P.S. Add a touch of yuzu kosho or grated ginger for extra flavor kick.

ASPARAGUS AND FRIED TOFU MISO SOUP

アスパラと揚げ豆腐の味噌汁

Springtime is asparagus season, which means (at least to us) it's time for asparagus miso soup. In this version the tender shoots are paired with fried tofu (*abura age*), creating a tasty contrast. The key here is to avoid overcooking the asparagus; you want it to retain a slight crunch and vibrant green color. Trim off the tough bottom ends before slicing. Experiment with other spring vegetables, if you desire, switching out the asparagus for snow peas, sugar snap peas, or broccoli. We think this soup is perfect just as it is, but if you're in the mood, add a flavor accent (see page 28).

SERVES 4

3 pieces fried tofu

4 cups dashi (page 40)

½ pound asparagus, trimmed and cut on the diagonal into ½-inch pieces

¼ cup shinshu miso

Place the fried tofu pieces in a colander in the sink. Pour boiling water over them to remove excess oil on both sides. Use chopsticks to press out excess water, then let the tofu sit until cool to the touch. Slice the tofu into thin strips and set aside.

In a medium saucepan, bring the dashi to a boil over medium heat. Reduce the heat so the liquid simmers. Add the asparagus and cook until it turns bright green, about 1 minute. Be careful not to overcook. Add the fried tofu strips and cook for another minute, until heated through.

To dissolve the miso, you have two choices: If you have a strainer that fits inside your saucepan, add the miso to the strainer and dunk it into the broth. Dissolve the miso with a spoon, pressing against the sides of the strainer. Or add the miso to a small bowl and pour in about ½ cup of the broth. Whisk to dissolve, then add the mixture back to the broth, stirring gently to combine. Simmer for 30 seconds to blend the flavors and harmonize the ingredients, but don't let the soup boil. Turn off the heat.

Ladle the soup into four bowls. Serve immediately.

S&B
SANSHO

BRUSSELS SPROUT MISO SOUP

芽キャベツの味噌汁

Brussels sprouts aren't an obvious veggie for the miso soup treatment, but Tadashi had this inspiration way back when he first encountered them in America. We love this soup for fall. The key is to slice the Brussels sprouts as thinly as possible so they quickly cook through in the soup. A speedy sauté before adding the dashi helps mellow any bitterness and brings out their natural sweetness, while the sesame oil adds its own beautiful flavor and aroma. We love the complex flavor of hatcho miso, which adds depth and umami to this satisfying soup. Try this method with thinly sliced cabbage or kale, too.

SERVES 4

1 tablespoon sesame oil

½ pound Brussels sprouts, trimmed, halved lengthwise, and thinly sliced

4 cups dashi (page 40)

¼ cup hatcho miso (or aka miso)

In a medium saucepan, combine the sesame oil and Brussels sprouts. Cook over medium heat, stirring frequently, until the Brussels sprouts become bright green and slightly softened, about 2 minutes. Add the dashi and bring to a boil. Reduce the heat and simmer for about 2 minutes.

To dissolve the miso, you have two choices: If you have a strainer that fits inside your saucepan, add the miso to the strainer and dunk it into the broth. Dissolve the miso with a spoon, pressing against the sides of the strainer. Or add the miso to a small bowl and pour in about ½ cup of the broth. Whisk to dissolve, then add the mixture back to the broth, stirring gently to combine. Simmer for 30 seconds to blend the flavors and harmonize the ingredients, but don't let the soup boil. Turn off the heat.

Ladle the soup into four bowls. Serve immediately.

ONiON AND POTATO MiSO SOUP

玉葱と馬鈴薯の味噌汁

This hearty winter soup is not just super satisfying; it's also a quick history lesson in a bowl, revealing how ingredients once foreign to Japan quickly found their way into traditional dishes. In the late nineteenth century an American agricultural expert named Professor William Smith Clark introduced dairy cattle to the far northern island of Hokkaido, leading to the adoption of milk, cheese, and butter in the Japanese diet. This soup reflects that culinary evolution, marrying a touch of velvety butter with potatoes and onions—roots also introduced to Hokkaido and once unknown in Japan. Creating an awase, or mixed, miso by blending varieties adds depth and complexity (you can do this for other miso soups, too). We like to leave the skin on the potatoes for their nutrients and earthy flavor, and sauté the onions first to coax out their natural sweetness. In Hokkaido, green cabbage is sometimes added to this soup, so try that if you'd like—just sauté it with the onions. (By the way, Professor Clark is still celebrated in Hokkaido with an annual Clark Day observance every April 16.)

SERVES 4

2 tablespoons unsalted butter

1 medium onion, thinly sliced (about ¼ pound)

1 pound new potatoes, cut in half lengthwise and sliced crosswise ¼ inch thick (no need to peel)

4 cups dashi (page 40)

¼ cup awase miso (equal parts aka and shiro miso mixed together)

In a medium saucepan, combine the butter and onions. Cook over medium heat, stirring frequently, until the onions turn translucent, about 2 minutes. Add the potatoes and cook for 3 more minutes, stirring occasionally, until the potatoes begin to soften. Stir gently so you don't break apart the potatoes.

Add the dashi and bring it to a boil. Reduce to a simmer and cook for 7 minutes, until the potatoes are tender (test by pushing a chopstick through a potato slice; it should go through easily).

To dissolve the miso, you have two choices: If you have a strainer that fits inside your saucepan, add the miso to the strainer and dunk it into the broth. Dissolve the miso with a spoon, pressing against the sides of the strainer. Or add the miso to a small bowl and pour in about ½ cup of the broth. Whisk to dissolve, then add the mixture back to the broth, stirring gently to combine. Simmer for 30 seconds to blend the flavors and harmonize the ingredients, but don't let the soup boil. Turn off the heat.

Ladle the soup into four bowls. Serve immediately.

P.S. For extra richness, add a small pat of butter to each bowl before serving. A touch of grated garlic or ginger can also add a nice zing to the soup.

KENCHIN JIRU

(VEGETARIAN TOFU SOUP)

けんちん汁

Kenchin jiru is a classic dish of *shojin ryori,* the traditional vegetarian cuisine of Zen Buddhist monks (see page 139). It checks all the satisfying plant-based boxes: root vegetables, mushrooms, tofu, and shiitake dashi. Interestingly, the tofu here is crumbled, and not for culinary reasons. According to legend (and we love legends), a young monk way back when at the Kencho-ji temple, not far from Tokyo, accidentally dropped a block of fresh tofu onto the kitchen floor. Rather than toss the broken tofu bits, he incorporated them into the temple's vegetable soup. (Hey, it's a Buddhist temple—the kitchen floor was immaculate.) Besides reflecting the foundational Japanese philosophy of *mottai-nai,* or "don't be wasteful," the crumbled tofu symbolizes the Zen belief in making the best use of available food and sharing it equally. Nourishment for the belly and soul, all in one bowl. Good work, monk!

SERVES 4

- ¼ pound burdock root
- 1 tablespoon sesame oil
- 1 small carrot, scrubbed, halved, and thinly sliced crosswise
- ¼ pound daikon, trimmed, quartered lengthwise, and thinly sliced crosswise
- ½ (14-ounce) package firm tofu, drained and crumbled
- 4 cups Shiitake Dashi (page 43)
- 3 tablespoons usukuchi soy sauce
- ¼ pound shiitake mushrooms, reserved from making the dashi, thinly sliced
- 2 tablespoons Shibori Scallions (page 41)
- 2 teaspoons freshly grated ginger

Fill a small bowl with cold water. Under cold running water, use steel wool or a scrubby to gently rub off the brown exterior of the burdock root until you see the pale white flesh (it doesn't have to be perfect). Thinly slice the burdock crosswise and place the slices in the bowl.

To a medium saucepan over medium heat, add the sesame oil. When the oil is hot, drain the burdock root and add it to the saucepan. Cook, stirring, for 1 minute. Add the carrot and cook for 1 minute, stirring frequently. Add the daikon and cook for 1 minute more, stirring frequently. Now add the crumbled tofu and cook, stirring frequently, for about 1 minute, just to heat through.

Pour in the shiitake dashi and the soy sauce and add the sliced shiitake mushrooms. Increase the heat to medium-high and bring the mixture to a boil. Reduce the heat and let simmer for about 5 minutes, until the vegetables are tender (test by pushing a chopstick through a daikon slice—it should slide through easily).

Ladle the soup into four bowls. Garnish with the shibori scallions and grated ginger. Serve immediately.

MISO SOUP WITH MUSSELS
ムール貝の味噌汁

Tadashi grew up in the Shitamachi neighborhood of Tokyo, a working class burg packed with carpenters, fishermen, miso makers, and other artisans—an area with its own singular subculture, dialect, and in-your-face attitude (think old-school Brooklyn). When Tadashi was a kid, fishmongers on bicycles squeezed through the busy streets singing "Asari-oh!" to hawk asari clams pulled fresh from Tokyo Bay—clams his mom snapped up to cook this fast and easy miso soup. (Fresh tofu, roasted sweet potatoes, and even pet goldfish were sold this way, too.) Asari clams might not be readily available so we substitute them with mussels, another incredibly flavorful bivalve. Keep the mussels in the fridge until you're ready to use them, and make sure to allow them to breathe (sealing them in a ziplock bag is a bad idea). Scrub the mussels with a brush to rid them of any dirt and sand, then pull off the beards (the fibrous strands hanging from the shell).

SERVES 4

2 cups dashi (page 40)

2 cups water

1 pound mussels, scrubbed and beards removed

1 tablespoon sesame oil

¼ cup aka miso

2 tablespoons chopped chives (cut into 1-inch pieces)

In a medium saucepan, bring the dashi and water to a boil over medium-high heat. Add the mussels and cook for 2 to 3 minutes, until the mussels open up (discard any mussels that do not open). Reduce the heat to bring the broth to a simmer.

To dissolve the miso, you have two choices: If you have a strainer that fits inside your saucepan, add the miso to the strainer and dunk it into the broth. Dissolve the miso with a spoon, pressing against the sides of the strainer. Or add the miso to a small bowl and pour in about ½ cup of the broth. Whisk to dissolve, then add the mixture back to the broth, stirring gently to combine. Simmer for 30 seconds to blend the flavors and harmonize the ingredients, but don't let the soup boil. Turn off the heat.

Ladle the soup into four bowls. Garnish with the chives and serve immediately.

VARIATION

For a more complex soup, Tadashi loves to cook this version: First, sauté ½ cup chopped onions in olive oil over medium heat until they're translucent. Stir in ½ cup chopped, super fresh tomato. Cook for 30 seconds, stirring constantly, then follow the recipe above from the beginning. While not traditional, the addition of tomato and onion to this soup adds beautiful layers of flavor.

A DOZEN MORE MISO SOUPS

Miso soup combinations are truly endless. Here are a dozen simple varieties to try—and to inspire your own miso soup creations. Experiment with different misos and *awase* combinations; cut ingredients into chopstick-friendly pieces; follow the general ratio of 4 cups dashi to ¼ cup miso; and don't forget to garnish. (And, hey, have your own favorite miso soup combos? Share them with us! Email at hello@japanesecomfortcooking.com or DM at @japanesecomfortcooking on Instagram.)

1. Corn, okra, and fried tofu; garnish with grated ginger
2. Yellow squash, Swiss chard, and mushrooms; garnish with red yuzu kosho
3. Kabocha squash and onions; garnish with grated ginger
4. Shiitake mushrooms and green cabbage; start by sautéing the cabbage in sesame oil
5. Taro, firm tofu, and spinach; garnish with green yuzu kosho
6. Sweet potato, carrots, and daikon
7. Wakame seaweed (see page 111), onions, and fried tofu
8. Cod, napa cabbage, and daikon
9. Clams and scallions; add a splash of sake
10. Oysters, wakame seaweed, and chives; garnish with karashi mustard (see page 248)
11. Chicken, carrots, and bok choy; start by sautéing the chicken in ginger and sesame oil
12. Ground pork, fried tofu, and eggplant; start by sautéing the pork in ginger and sesame oil

TONJiRU

(PORK AND VEGETABLE MISO SOUP)

豚汁

Like Onion and Potato Miso Soup (page 48), this delicious bowl packs in a fascinating origin story. *Tonjiru,* which literally means "pork soup," became popular in the late nineteenth century, when the government began promoting a new and exciting health food—meat. Up to that point, the Japanese diet mostly consisted of vegetables, rice, and fish, but around that time Europeans and Americans began to appear in Japan—and guess what they ate? As tonjiru's popularity grew, regional variations appeared, our favorite being sukii-jiru, or "skiing soup," which was invented at—you guessed it—a ski resort. We're not really sure what made it unique, but who doesn't want to chow down on a dish called skiing soup? Okay, a few notes: If you can't find burdock for this recipe, just add more of the other roots (these soups are flexible). The recipe calls for water in addition to dashi because you're essentially creating a beautiful stock when you cook all the ingredients together so you don't need full-on dashi. And we're not using shibori scallions this time—you want the bite of raw scallions to contrast with the richness of the pork-infused stock.

SERVES 4

1 teaspoon rice vinegar

¼ pound burdock root

1 tablespoon sesame oil, plus extra for drizzling

1 pound thinly sliced fresh pork belly (found in Asian markets), cut into roughly 1-inch pieces

1 small carrot, scrubbed and thinly sliced into coins

½ pound daikon, peeled, quartered, and thinly sliced

2 cups dashi (page 40)

2 cups water

½ pound taro root (about 5 small pieces), peeled, cut into ½-inch slices, soaked in cold water and drained

¼ cup shiro miso (see page 20)

¼ cup thinly sliced scallions

1 tablespoon toasted black sesame seeds (or white, if you can't find them)

Fill a bowl with cold water and the vinegar. Under cold running water, use steel wool or a scrubby to gently rub off the brown outside skin of the burdock root until you see the pale white flesh (it doesn't have to be perfect). Thinly slice and add to the bowl; the vinegar will help the burdock retain its color and release bitterness. Set aside.

To a large saucepan over medium heat, add the sesame oil. When the oil is hot, add the pork belly and cook, stirring occasionally, until it is no longer pink and some of the fat has rendered, about 2 minutes.

CONTINUED →

TONJIRU, CONTINUED

Drain the burdock root and add it to the saucepan, along with the carrots. Cook, stirring occasionally, for about 3 minutes, until the vegetables begin to soften. Add the daikon and cook for 2 more minutes.

Add the dashi and water and bring to a boil over high heat. Reduce the heat to a simmer and add the drained taro. Cook, skimming any scum that appears on the surface, until the vegetables are tender, about 10 minutes. (To test, push a chopstick through the daikon and taro—it should slide through easily.)

To dissolve the miso, you have two choices: If you have a strainer that fits inside your saucepan, add the miso to the strainer and dunk it into the broth. Dissolve the miso with a spoon, pressing against the sides of the strainer. Or add the miso to a small bowl and pour in about ½ cup of the broth. Whisk to dissolve, then add the mixture to the broth, stirring gently to combine. Simmer for 30 seconds to blend the flavors and harmonize the ingredients, but don't let the soup boil. Turn off the heat.

Ladle the soup into four bowls, making sure each bowl gets a generous portion of pork and vegetables. Garnish with scallions and sesame seeds. Drizzle a little sesame oil over the garnish and serve immediately.

KASUJIRU

(SALMON AND SAKE KASU SOUP)

粕汁

Let's talk sake for a minute. Don't worry, we'll get back to soup shortly! A by-product of brewing sake is the mash, from which the liquid that we drink is squeezed out. But that mash isn't trash; it's a remarkable ingredient in its own right called *sake kasu*. (Mottai-nai again! See page 49.) Sake kasu is packed with a deep sake-infused flavor and pairs beautifully with salmon, the other star of this soup. (Back to soup!) *Saikyo* miso, a lightly fermented miso from Kyoto, adds a mellow sweetness for balance. Hailing from Japan's sake-producing regions, this soup is traditionally enjoyed in the winter, sake's brewing season. You can find sake kasu at Japanese markets, sometimes in the freezer section.

SERVES 4

- 4 ounces sake kasu
- ½ cup boiling water, plus more for rinsing the salmon
- 1 pound boneless salmon fillet (preferably with the skin on), cut into ¾-inch-thick slices
- 4 cups dashi (page 40)
- ½ pound daikon, peeled, quartered, and thinly sliced
- 1 teaspoon salt
- 2 tablespoons saikyo miso
- ½ pound napa cabbage, roughly chopped
- 2 tablespoons Shibori Scallions (page 41)
- 2 teaspoons freshly grated ginger

In a medium bowl, add the sake kasu and pour ½ cup boiling water over it. This will soften the sake kasu and make it easier to use. Set aside.

Place a colander in the sink. Put the salmon slices skin-side up in the colander and pour boiling water over them to remove any fishiness. Flip the slices over and repeat.

In a medium saucepan, bring the dashi to a boil over medium-high heat. Add the daikon and cook for about 5 minutes, until starting to soften. Reduce the heat to a simmer.

Drain the sake kasu and add it to the soup. Stir to dissolve, then add the salt. To dissolve the miso, you have two choices: If you have a strainer that fits inside your saucepan, add the miso to the strainer and dunk it into the broth. Dissolve the miso with a spoon, pressing against the sides of the strainer. Or add the miso to a small bowl and pour in about ½ cup of the broth. Whisk to dissolve, then add the mixture back to the broth, stirring gently to combine.

Add the napa cabbage and the salmon slices to the soup. Simmer for about 3 minutes, until the cabbage is tender and the fish is cooked through. Turn off the heat.

Ladle the soup into four bowls, making sure each bowl gets a generous portion of salmon and vegetables. Garnish with the shibori scallions and ginger. Serve immediately.

2

RICE

米

Rice is the bedrock of Japanese cuisine—and culture. It's so fundamental to the cooking that the Japanese term for a meal is *gohan,* which means "steamed rice."

Rice cultivation has informed the very foundations of Japanese culture since ancient times. The thing about growing rice is that you can't do it alone. It literally takes a village to manage irrigation, flood the paddies, till the paddies, drain the paddies, and harvest the crop. Hate your neighbors? Tough you-know-what. Suck it up and work together, or everyone starves. Facts. Even today, this reality continues to shape how the Japanese deal with each other: group harmony, consensus seeking, and conflict avoidance remain key characteristics of the culture.

Rice also plays a profound role in Japan's Shinto and Buddhist faiths. It's considered a symbol of prosperity and the force of life; it's central to ceremonies from New Year's to weddings to funerals. Every Japanese kid is taught that eighty-eight gods live inside each grain of rice, so don't waste a grain!

Japanese rice is a unique cultivar called Japonica, of which there are some three hundred varieties grown in Japan (*Koshihikari* being the most famous). The grains are short and plump, becoming moist and sticky when cooked owing to their high starch content. What about the flavor? The first thing that hits you when you eat freshly steamed Japanese rice is—wow, this tastes amazing! It has a beautiful aroma and is sweeter and more "ricey" (Is that a word?) than other varieties you may be used to. This is especially true of fresh-crop rice, i.e., grains that have been recently harvested.

(When Tadashi's mom cooked rice for breakfast early in the morning when he was a kid, the seductive aroma would waft over him and pull him out of bed like a Siren's call . . . who could sleep through *that*?)

You can buy fantastic Japanese rice, including fresh crop, via imported Japanese brands or from growers in places like California and Arkansas. Look for it in Asian markets and online. And don't be intimidated: Cooking Japanese rice is easy and straightforward—just measure, rinse, steep, and cook. Tadashi's "perfect" method (see page 60) explains how.

(At *ryotei,* or traditional Japanese fine-dining establishments, preparing rice *is* difficult as it becomes elevated to high art. Cooks carefully balance the weight of rice and water, even taking into account the weather and ambient humidity's effect on this ratio, as well as on steeping time. So precise and so fascinating. In fact, the traditional first step of a ryotei cook's apprenticeship—which can last up to eight years—is mastering the art of rice.)

When you cook rice, cook a ton of it! Rice freezes really well, so portion and freeze leftover rice, then quickly reheat it in the microwave or in a covered pot on low heat with a teaspoon of water. And with Japanese cooking, rice is a *must* with every meal—even with noodles. It might seem like carb overload, but walk into any ramen joint in Japan and you'll spy patrons inhaling bowls of rice on the side. *Gohan* means "meal" for a reason.

Finally, don't forget your *shamoji* when preparing rice. A shamoji is a flat paddle designed specifically for mixing and scooping rice. It's worth owning. Typically made from bamboo or wood (though you can find nonstick plastic models, too), it doesn't mush or cut the cooked grains like a metal spoon can. Dip it in water before scooping, so the rice doesn't stick to it.

HOW TO WASH RICE

Start by adding the rice to a large bowl. Place the bowl in the sink and pour in just enough cold water to cover the rice. Swirl the rice around with your hand for 5 to 10 seconds. As soon as the water becomes milky and opaque, quickly drain the rice. This first rinse removes surface starch and impurities.

Refill the bowl with water and gently rub the rice grains with your hand for about 30 seconds. Be careful not to break the grains; this is a delicate motion. Drain the rice again.

Repeat this process of washing and draining until the water becomes clear, usually about three times. (By "clear" we mean the water is a lot less cloudy and you can see the rice; we're not talking clear like a spring-fed mountain stream.) After the final rinse, drain the rice in a colander.

TADASHI'S PERFECT STEAMED RICE

白飯

So you want to make perfect rice at home? You have two choices: Drop a bag of ducats for a high-tech "fuzzy logic" Japanese rice cooker—or listen to your Uncle Tadashi! Seriously, after cooking professionally for three-plus decades, Tadashi has distilled a method for cooking consistent, fluffy, glossy, amazing rice at home. Before we get into the nitty-gritty, let's talk bigger concepts: First step is "washing" the rice. What does that mean? Washing is more like delicately massaging the rice, rubbing the grains together to polish them and remove surface starch. Next, soaking the rice allows the dry grains to absorb just enough moisture to cook evenly, as heat travels through vapor (steam). Now on to the cooking part: You'll see that we start with high heat, then lower it for the bulk of the cooking. This is key. Boiling the rice hard at the beginning kickstarts the vapor journey through the grains; lowering the heat continues the cooking without burning the rice. This is basically how the pros cook rice in Japanese restaurant kitchens (but with many more subtleties, see page 58). The result is perfect rice that clumps together in classic Japanese rice style but is not wet or mushy; rice that expresses the grain's beautiful, sublime flavor. Now to the nitty-gritty: Like everything else worthwhile in life, effort is the point. In other words, you have to practice cooking rice. After a few tries you'll start to understand how it works.

SERVES 4

2 cups Japanese short-grain rice

2 cups water

Wash and soak the rice following the method on page 59. Add the drained rice and 2 cups water to a medium saucepan and let steep for 30 minutes. This allows the rice to absorb moisture and ensures even cooking.

Bring the rice to a boil over medium-high heat, uncovered. Reduce the heat to medium, cover, and let the rice boil for 5 minutes. Reduce the heat again, this time to very low, and let the rice cook for 10 minutes. Do not lift the lid during this entire process, as the steam necessary for perfect cooking will escape. (Trust the process!)

Turn off the heat and let the rice sit, still covered, for an additional 10 minutes to finish cooking. This resting period allows the rice to firm up and absorb any remaining moisture.

Fluff the rice gently with a shamoji or fork, being careful not to break the grains. Serve immediately.

P.S. Depending on your burner, the rice might form a thin amber crust as it rests called *okoge*. People in Japan separate it from the white rice and enjoy it on its own.

JAPANESE BROWN RICE

(GENMAI)

玄米

Brown rice is rice with the bran and germ intact, as opposed to white rice where the bran and germ are milled off (brown rice gets its signature hue from the beige bran). Brown rice has a lovely nutty flavor and the germ is packed with nutrients. Tadashi's perfect rice cooking method works perfectly here too, but with a couple of adjustments. First, because the grains are encased in bran, you don't have to wash them as much, but you do have to soak them much more, for two hours, so plan ahead. (The washing water won't get as milky as with white rice, by the way.) And you'll cook this rice with more water and for a longer duration, all to give the water vapor more opportunity to work its steamy magic on the grains and transform them into something tender and delicious.

SERVES 4

2 cups Japanese short-grain brown rice

3 cups water

Wash and soak the rice. Start by adding the rice to a large bowl. Fill the bowl with water and gently rub the rice grains with your hand for about 30 seconds. Be careful not to break the grains—this is a delicate motion. Drain the rice. Repeat this process of washing and draining two times.

Drain the rice in a colander. Add the drained rice and 3 cups water to a medium saucepan and let steep for 2 hours. This allows the rice to absorb moisture and ensures even cooking.

Bring the rice to a boil over medium-high heat, uncovered. Reduce the heat to medium, cover, and let the rice boil for 5 minutes. Reduce the heat again, this time to very low, and let it cook for 25 minutes. Do not lift the lid during the entire 30-minute cooking time, as the steam necessary for perfect cooking will escape. (Trust the process!)

Turn off the heat and let the rice sit, still covered, for an additional 10 minutes to finish cooking. This resting period allows the rice to firm up and absorb any remaining moisture.

Fluff the rice gently with a shamoji or fork, being careful not to break the grains. Serve immediately.

TAMAGO KAKE GOHAN A.K.A. "TKG"

卵掛けご飯

This is an insanely easy recipe to make, but it's deep! So deep, in fact, that this traditional dish has been designated by UNESCO as an "intangible cultural heritage" and is the focus of festivals and events, including something called the Tamago Kake Gohan Symposium. So what are we talking about? Freshly cooked rice; incredibly fresh, raw eggs; and traditionally brewed tamari soy sauce (see page 19). That's it. Swirl them all together and you've got *TKG* (in Japan it's actually called "tee-kay-gee," like the English letters). And with just those three ingredients, TKG expresses everything that is so mind-blowing about Japanese cuisine—the simplicity, the balance, the reliance on natural flavors. Tadashi grew up eating TKG, which for him symbolizes family togetherness. Harris, who loves the rural corners of Japan, can tell you about the TKG he ate for breakfast in the snowy mountains of Akita, on a farm in Kyushu, along the pilgrim's trail in Shikoku, and more (ask him). If you raise chickens or live near a farmers' market or farms, grab some super fresh eggs and make TKG for breakfast. If you'd like, add chopped scallions or *natto* (fermented soybeans, funky and sticky, but so nutty and delicious). Mix everything together and eat. The steaming hot rice will cook the egg ever so slightly, which also adds to the flavor experience.

SERVES 4

4 cups hot, freshly cooked Japanese short-grain rice

4 eggs

2 tablespoons plus 2 teaspoons tamari soy sauce

For each serving, add 1 cup of the rice to a bowl, crack an egg over it and drizzle with 2 teaspoons tamari. Mix with chopsticks until the egg is fully incorporated and the rice turns creamy. Serve immediately.

P.S. If you prefer, replace the raw eggs with soft-boiled (see page 68) or poached (see page 96) eggs, or *Onsen Tamago* (see page 96), which is also yummy!

SHIOZAKE ONIGIRI
(BROILED SALMON RICE BALLS)
焼塩鮭おにぎり

Although they date back more than two thousand years in Japanese food culture, *onigiri*, or "rice balls," are having a moment these days. Over millennia, onigiri, which—like TKG (see page 63)—are designated as an "intangible cultural heritage" by UNESCO, were served as meals for the royal court, chow for farmers, military rations for samurai, nineteenth-century school lunch, carbs for the first *ekiben* (train station boxed meals), and on and on. But when people realized they could wolf down an onigiri with one hand while doom-scrolling Instagram with the other, well, all bets were off. There are tons of varieties of onigiri, and lots of different shapes, from the traditional triangle to a literal ball. Here we offer onigiri filled with salted salmon, but you can also use umeboshi (see page 249), mentaiko (salted, spicy cod roe), kombu tsukudani (see page 71), or even canned tuna mixed with mayo. This recipe makes four large onigiri, but feel free to form smaller ones instead.

SERVES 4

4 cups cooked Japanese short-grain rice (freshly cooked or reheated)

1 teaspoon salt

4 ounces Broiled Salted Salmon (recipe follows), shredded

2 sheets nori, each cut into half (each sheet is about 8 by 7 inches)

In a large bowl, combine the hot (or warm) rice and salt and mix gently.

Using 1 cup cooked rice per serving, add the rice to a small bowl (like a cereal bowl) just big enough to hold it. Jiggle the bowl, moving in a flat, circular motion, like the motion of a hula hoop, until the rice forms a ball on its own—a neat kitchen trick Tadashi's mom taught him. This motion packs the rice so it holds together.

Make a small indentation in the center of the rice ball with your thumb. Place 1 ounce of the cooked salmon (or your preferred filling) into the indentation. Carefully press the rice around the filling to cover it completely.

Wet your hands and place the ball of rice between your cupped palms. Now squeeze, flip, and turn the rice ball several times to form it into a triangular shape (see page 67). This motion takes a little practice but after a few onigiri, you'll get the hang of it. Avoid packing the rice too tightly; you want it to just stick together.

Wrap a half sheet of nori around the rice and serve. (Top the onigiri with a few flakes of salmon if you like.) Repeat this process for the remaining servings.

BROILED SALTED SALMON

焼塩鮭

Use farmed or wild salmon to make this very traditional *shiozake,* as it's called in Japan.

SERVES 4

½ pound skin-on salmon fillet

Kosher salt

Divide the salmon into four portions and place on a sheet pan. Generously season with salt on all sides, using enough to cover the surface.

Let the salted salmon sit at room temperature for 1 hour. This allows the salt to penetrate the salmon, enhancing its flavor, expelling moisture, and firming up the texture. After 1 hour, use a paper towel to gently wipe off any excess salt and moisture from the salmon pieces.

Preheat a broiler. Place the salmon skin-side down on a foil-lined sheet pan. Broil for about 5 minutes on one side. Carefully flip the salmon pieces using a fish spatula and broil for another 5 minutes on the other side, or until the salmon is cooked through and the skin has a beautiful golden color.

Let the salmon cool before shredding it for the onigiri or Chazuke (page 70) recipes, including the skin if you desire (we love the skin).

HOW TO FORM ONIGIRI

KAYU WITH DASHI AND SOFT-BOILED EGG

(RICE PORRIDGE)

だし掛け粥と半熟卵

Back in the aughts, Harris was invited to train for a month in the kitchen of Hyotei in Kyoto. Hyotei is not just any restaurant. Founded as a teahouse along a pilgrim's trail 450 years ago, it was converted into a full-fledged restaurant in 1837. It's run by the fifteenth generation of the wonderful Takahashi family, stewards of one of Japan's true cultural treasures. The restaurant serves traditional kaiseki meals in centuries-old, thatched-roof teahouses arrayed along a narrow stream, where the muffled sounds of rushing water become the soundtrack for an astonishing procession of dishes presented on exquisite lacquer trays and sampled while sitting cross-legged on tatami. For Harris, it was a full-on immersion into Japanese food culture, and a dream come true (plus a lot of hard work). Interestingly, for a restaurant this hallowed, its signature dishes are super simple, including this one: a soft-boiled egg (the famous "Hyotei egg," which has been on the menu for almost two centuries) and *kayu,* or "rice porridge." What more do you need to know about Japanese cuisine? The eggs, which have been sourced for generations from the same farms and are precisely cooked until their bright orange yolks are perfectly creamy, adorn rice porridge cooked from scratch. (Guess who peeled hundreds of these eggs?) We can't promise Hyotei eggs, but kayu is totally achievable at home. This old-school dish will warm your belly and soul any time of the year. Give it a go. Besides the beautiful soft-boiled egg, we drizzle a traditional dashi sauce over the porridge to add delicate umami flavor, just like they do at Hyotei.

SERVES 4

½ cup Japanese short-grain rice

3 cups water

4 eggs

Salt

2 teaspoons wasabi (optional)

DASHI SAUCE

½ cup dashi (see page 40)

1 tablespoon usukuchi soy sauce

1 tablespoon mirin

1 teaspoon potato starch (katakuriko)

1 tablespoon warm water

In a medium saucepan, wash the rice and then soak it in 3 cups water, following Tadashi's Perfect Steamed Rice (page 60) recipe.

While the rice is soaking, prepare the soft-boiled eggs by placing a small saucepan of water over high heat. Add a healthy pinch of salt to the water. This allows the water to reach its boiling point faster and helps seal cracks that could develop in the shells as the eggs cook. When the water is boiling, add the eggs. Use a spoon or chopsticks to swirl them in the water for about 1 minute so the yolks set in the center of the eggs and look pretty—this also makes the eggs easier to peel. Boil the eggs over medium heat for exactly 7 minutes in total. While the eggs are cooking, fill a bowl with cold water. When the eggs are ready,

HAIGA RICE

You know white rice. You know brown rice. Now meet *haiga* rice (*haiga mai*). While white rice has the bran and germ milled off and brown rice retains both, with haiga rice, the bran is removed but the germ remains intact. So what's the big deal about that? Rice germ is loaded with important vitamins and nutrients, and even high levels of something called GABA, which can help you sleep better and reduce anxiety(!). In fact, way back in 1928 the Japanese government recommended replacing white rice with haiga because of its many nutritional benefits. But producers ultimately enriched white rice with vitamins, so haiga never caught on. In recent years, people have rediscovered haiga and its natural nutritional benefits. And because the nutty-flavored bran is removed, haiga tastes more like white rice than brown. Best of all, you cook it exactly like you would white rice—in other words, quickly (just follow Tadashi's instructions on page 60). Give it a try!

transfer them to the bowl and shock them with the cold water, which will help them peel easier. When cool enough to handle, peel the eggs, slice in half lengthwise, and set aside.

Bring the rice to a boil over medium-high heat. Reduce the heat to low and cover, but leave the lid open a crack to allow steam to escape. Cook for 1 hour, gently stirring every 15 minutes so the rice on the bottom doesn't burn. When most of the liquid is gone and you have a glutinous, glossy porridge, with the rice cooked through but not mushy, the kayu is ready.

While the kayu is cooking, prepare the dashi sauce. In a small saucepan, bring the dashi, usukuchi, and mirin to a boil over medium heat. Reduce the heat to low. Meanwhile, in a small bowl, mix together the potato starch and water to create a slurry. Pour the slurry into the simmering liquid, stirring constantly for 15 to 30 seconds, until it thickens. Remove from the heat.

When the kayu has finished cooking, remove it from the heat, placing the saucepan on a silpat or towel on the counter. Now fully cover the saucepan with the lid and let the porridge rest for 10 minutes; this allows the rice to finish cooking. When it's ready, gently mix the porridge from the bottom, being careful not to break the grains of rice.

To serve, divide the porridge among four bowls. Drizzle the dashi sauce over the rice and top each with an egg and a small mound of wasabi, if you desire. Serve immediately.

CHAZUKE

(SOUPY RICE IN GREEN TEA)

茶漬け

This versatile dish, which traces its origins back more than a thousand years, has served as an easy breakfast; a classic late-night snack for students cramming for exams; a final dish traditionally presented in Kyoto to dinner guests as a not-so-subtle signal to hit the bricks; and even a tried-and-true hangover helper. Samurai ate it before battle, and specialized chazuke shops—an early version of fast food—popped up during the Edo Period (1603–1868). Chazuke has three ingredients: cooked rice, green tea poured over said rice, and various toppings and seasonings sprinkled over it. This soupy rice is so simple and fast—you're just assembling ingredients—but so comforting and soothing. We offer this recipe adorned with broiled salted salmon and *bubu arare* (tiny rice crackers with a fun name!), but you can try other classic toppings like *umeboshi* (salted, pickled ume fruit, a kind of apricot), kombu tsukudani (recipe follows), mentaiko (salted marinated cod roe), natto (fermented soybeans), or shredded nori. Chazuke for the soul . . .

SERVES 4

4 cups cooked Japanese short-grain rice, warm

Broiled Salted Salmon (page 66), shredded

2 cups hot sencha (Japanese green tea; see Note)

4 teaspoons soy sauce

1 sheet nori, torn into small pieces

4 teaspoons bubu arare

2 teaspoons wasabi (optional)

Have ready four bowls. Assemble each bowl as follows: Add 1 cup rice and top with a portion of the salmon (we include the skin—it adds wonderful flavor). Pour ½ cup sencha and 1 teaspoon soy sauce over the rice and salmon. Top with torn nori, bubu arare, and a small mound of wasabi, if desired. Serve immediately.

NOTE

Steep the sencha in water heated between 158°F and 176°F (taste what works best for your tea). Don't use full-on boiling water, which will cause this tea to taste astringent and bitter.

KOMBU TSUKUDANI

昆布佃煮

Tsukudani is a simple method for naturally preserving ingredients by simmering them in soy sauce and sugar, transforming them into something sweet-savory and bold. It's a delicious, traditional condiment used for rice dishes like chazuke, onigiri, kayu, or even plain rice and is also sampled on its own to wake up the palate when you're drinking sake. Here we make it with leftover kombu from cooking dashi—a classic preparation that expresses the foundational Japanese philosophy of mottai-nai, or minimizing waste. Tsukudani can also be prepared with leftover katsuobushi or shiitake from dashi making (or a combo of dashi ingredients); tiny sardines (*shirasu*), shrimp, ginger, or whole peppercorns; and, in some regions of Japan, even walnuts, bee larvae, or calcium-rich grasshoppers.

MAKES ABOUT 1 CUP

1 cup cooked kombu from dashi (see page 40), cut into roughly ½-inch squares

¼ cup soy sauce

2 tablespoons sake

2 tablespoons sugar

2 tablespoons water

1 teaspoon sesame seeds

In a medium saucepan, add all the ingredients and bring to a boil over medium-high heat. Reduce the heat to low and a simmer until the liquid has almost completely evaporated, about 10 minutes. Stir occasionally so the bottom doesn't burn. You want about 1 tablespoon of liquid to remain.

Allow the tsukudani to cool to room temperature before using. You can keep tsukudani in the refrigerator for up to a month.

TORI TAKIKOMI GOHAN

(CHICKEN MIXED RICE)

鶏炊き込み飯

Takikomi gohan, or mixed rice, is a Japanese cooking standard that's delicious, nutritious, and irresistible. Every region, and even individual families, has its own beloved version. Here we prepare a classic mixed rice with chicken, shiitake, and root veggies. The burdock adds a beautiful earthiness that complements the chicken, and instead of water we use shiitake dashi for its own flavor and umami boost. This dish can easily be made vegetarian by subbing the chicken with more of the roots. We add less liquid to the rice than when cooking steamed rice because the soy sauce, mirin, and the natural moisture found from the vegetables and protein contribute additional liquid. Mixed rice is super flexible. If you don't have, say, burdock, just skip it or add something else: abura age (fried tofu), hijiki (soak first, see page 116), or fresh mixed Japanese mushrooms.

SERVES 4

2 cups Japanese short-grain rice

1½ cups Shiitake Dashi (page 43)

2 tablespoons soy sauce

2 tablespoons mirin

½ teaspoon salt

½ pound boneless, skinless chicken thighs or leg meat, cut into bite-size pieces

4 reconstituted shiitake mushrooms, from the dashi, chopped

2 tablespoons diced carrot

¼ cup chopped burdock root (about 2 ounces; see Tonjiru, page 52, for cleaning instructions)

¼ cup thinly sliced scallions

Sansho (optional)

In a medium saucepan, wash the rice and then soak it for 30 minutes in the shiitake dashi, following Tadashi's Perfect Steamed Rice (page 60) recipe.

Add the soy sauce, mirin, and salt to the saucepan with the rice and gently mix to combine the seasonings. Lay the chicken, shiitake, carrot, and burdock root on top of the rice but do not mix. This is important because if you mix the ingredients with the rice, the rice will not be able to steam evenly and you'll have clumps of undercooked rice.

Bring the rice to a boil, uncovered, over medium-high heat. Reduce the heat to medium, cover, and let the rice boil for 5 minutes. Reduce the heat again, this time to very low, and let it cook for 10 minutes. Do not lift the lid during this entire process, as the steam necessary for perfect cooking will escape. (Trust the process!)

Turn off the heat and let the rice sit, covered, for an additional 10 minutes to finish cooking. This resting period allows the rice to firm up and absorb any remaining moisture.

Use a shamoji or a large wooden spoon to gently mix all the ingredients together and fluff the rice, being careful not to break the grains. Serve immediately, garnished with the scallions and sprinkled with sansho, if desired.

TAMAGO YAKI MESHI

(EGG FRIED RICE)

卵焼き飯

Like with Tadashi's Perfect Steamed Rice on page 60, here we share, basically, Tadashi's perfect Japanese-style fried rice. You can't go wrong with this method. This dish, also known as *chahan,* uses leftover rice and cooks hot—and fast. Watch a few wok-cooking videos on YouTube to get hyped up! Woks are great, but a cast-iron, carbon steel, or quality nonstick skillet works fine too. (We used Harris's trusty 11-inch cast-iron Lodge skillet to cook this dish.) Okay, so you might be wondering: What's the difference between Japanese fried rice and its famous Chinese cousin—the global fried-rice standard? The Japanese variety uses less soy sauce, resulting in a lighter color and milder flavor, and relies on Japanese short-grain rice as well as local ingredients like shiitake and kakuni (lots of other ingredients work too; see the list on page 77). But ultimately, this dish is, in fact, an adaptation of Chinese fried rice, which was introduced to Japan in the 1860s by Chinese immigrants and evolved from there. Some practical considerations: If you don't happen to own a *chuan* (a special Chinese wok spatula), use a big ol' cooking spoon to turn the rice; you'll be stirring throughout the cooking. Make sure to ventilate, because it could get smoky. And remember, *hayai*—move quickly!

SERVES 4

2 tablespoons toasted sesame oil

3 eggs, beaten

2 cups cooked Japanese short-grain white rice, warm (leftover rice is fine; microwave it if cold)

1 tablespoon sake

1 tablespoon soy sauce

Pinch of salt

¼ teaspoon ground white pepper

¼ cup chopped scallions, plus 2 tablespoons for garnish

1 tablespoon toasted sesame seeds

Preheat a large skillet (cast-iron or stainless steel is ideal) over medium-high heat. You want the skillet really hot. (If using stainless steel, test by dripping a few drops of water onto the surface of the skillet. If the water beads then vaporizes—instead of just sizzling—the skillet is ready.)

Add the sesame oil. It will immediately start to smoke. Coat the surface with the oil, then quickly add the eggs. The eggs will immediately begin to bubble rapidly. Cook for about 10 seconds, then dump the rice over the eggs. The eggs will still be uncooked on top—that's fine. Now, use your cooking spoon to mix the egg and rice together and break up any clumps. This action will coat the rice with uncooked egg, which will prevent the grains from sticking to each other—you don't want clumpy fried rice. Stir constantly for about 30 seconds. Add the sake, soy sauce, salt, and white pepper. Keep stirring. Add the scallions. Stir for about 1½ minutes more and remove from the heat.

Divide the rice among four bowls, garnish with the additional scallions and the sesame seeds, and serve immediately.

TAKO MESHi

(OCTOPUS MIXED RICE)

蛸飯

Who knew a trip to Costco could inspire a Japanese dish? When Tadashi's wife returned home from a run to the retail behemoth, she surprised him with something that stopped him in his tracks: perfectly tender, flash-frozen octopus. When he first arrived in America back in the 1980s, you couldn't even find octopus on a sushi bar menu. Now it's at Costco. That's progress! The Costco octopus evoked, for him, memories of his mom cooking tako meshi, or octopus mixed rice. This one-pot wonder is a Japanese comfort food classic, originally evolving from a need to use up leftover ingredients (the fundamental philosophy of mottai-nai—avoiding waste—popping up again!). The recipe can also be prepared with squid, scallops, shrimp, salmon, white-fleshed fish like cod, or even thinly sliced chicken or pork. (But frozen cooked octopus is now fairly easy to find, and not just at Costco, so make sure to try it!) The secret here is the natural flavor of the main ingredients blending with traditional umami-powered seasonings, and infusing all that lip-smacking goodness into the rice. A lot happening under the pot cover, but as per usual with Japanese cooking, it's straightforward and easy to execute.

SERVES 4

2 cups Japanese short-grain rice

1 cup dashi (see page 40)

½ cup water

2 tablespoons mirin

2 tablespoons usukuchi soy sauce

¾ pound cooked octopus, defrosted if frozen, cut into ½-inch cubes

1 tablespoon thinly sliced ginger

1 tablespoon thinly sliced shiso leaves

In a medium saucepan, wash the rice and then soak it for 30 minutes in the dashi and water, following Tadashi's Perfect Steamed Rice (page 60) recipe.

To the same saucepan, add the mirin and soy sauce and gently mix to combine. Scatter the octopus and ginger over the rice without stirring. (If you mix in the octopus and ginger before cooking, it will interfere with the circulating steam that transmits heat to the rice grains, and the rice won't cook properly.)

Bring the rice to a boil, uncovered, over medium-high heat. Reduce the heat to medium, cover, and let the rice boil for 5 minutes. Reduce the heat again, this time to very low, and let the rice cook for 10 minutes. Do not lift the lid during the 15-minute cooking time, as the steam necessary for perfect cooking will escape. (Trust the process!)

Turn off the heat and let the rice sit, covered, for an additional 10 minutes to finish cooking. This resting period allows the rice to firm up and absorb any remaining moisture. After resting, gently fluff the rice with a rice paddle or fork, distributing the

ADDITIONAL INGREDIENTS FOR FRIED RICE

With Japanese fried rice you generally want to use one additional ingredient, not a bunch. Add the ingredient right after you add the rice. Adjust the cooking time by 1 to 2 minutes to heat it through.

Try our fried rice recipe (page 74) with 2 to 3 ounces of:

- Kakuni (braised pork belly, page 239)
- Crispy bacon, crumbled
- Baked ham, cut into bite-size cubes
- Roasted chicken (see page 205), cut into bite-size cubes
- Cooked shrimp, chopped
- Canned tuna, drained and flaked
- Cooked vegetables like corn, asparagus, green peas, or sugar snap peas, cut into bite-size pieces where appropriate
- Also, you can add chopped garlic or ginger, to taste.

octopus and ginger throughout. Replace the lid and let sit for an additional 5 minutes to allow the flavors to meld. Serve the tako meshi in individual bowls, garnished with the shiso leaves.

Leftover tako meshi (if there's such a thing!) can be formed into onigiri (see page 67) or refrigerated or frozen to save for another meal. Allow the onigiri to come to room temperature before eating (you can microwave it if frozen).

3

NOODLES

麺

Noodles are the beating heart of Japanese comfort cooking, with at least sixty thousand dedicated noodles shops dotting a country a tad smaller than California. And beyond sit-down (and stand-up) joints, noodles are a go-to grab at *konbini* (page 103) and, happily, a beloved home-cooking standard. Broadly, we're talking about soba, somen, udon, and ramen, which are slurped down for breakfast, lunch, dinner, late-night nosh, or a midday refuel. Don't be surprised to pass ramen joints in Tokyo with lines snaking up the block—at eight in the morning!

Noodles arrived in Japan around the ninth and tenth centuries. Originally, they were luxury eats for aristocrats. By the twelfth century, soba became a staple for samurai. Five hundred years later, both soba and udon evolved into popular street food. Interestingly, soba, whose preparation is now akin to high art, was considered a poor person's food compared with udon. That attitude started to shift in the late eighteenth century as the people of Edo (today's Tokyo) began to appreciate the toothsome noodle's subtle aroma and slurpability (it's important to slurp!). By the late nineteenth century, Chinese immigrants arrived and introduced ramen, derived from Chinese *la mian* ("pulled noodles"), which quickly rocketed in popularity—a wild noodle ride that continues to this day. Just ask any ramen otaku, or "ramen obsessive."

Soba is rolled from buckwheat flour (for more on soba, see page 82), while somen, udon, and ramen are wheat-based. Somen are thin and vermicelli-like and cook superfast; they're the quintessential noodles of summer. Udon are generally thick, chewy noodles that you traditionally knead by stomping on the dough with your sock-covered feet; while with ramen, wheat flour is mixed with *kansui* (alkaline) to give the noodles their trademark yellowish color, taste, and springy texture. Each of these noodle types comes in many varieties. For ramen alone, there are hundreds of hyper-local styles across Japan.

While the pros will spend long hours (even days) teasing a ramen broth from pork and/or chicken bones, in the recipes that follow, we share our favorite homey versions you'll crush in no time, whatever your personal noodle jam. And, oh, last thing: These dishes are *flexible*. We offer loads of variations, as per usual, but don't hesitate to whip up your own bespoke twists!

RAMEN
FRESH RAMEN
UDON
SOMEN AND SOBA
FROZEN COOKED UDON
KISHIMEN

KiNOKO SOBA

(MUSHROOM SOBA)

木の子蕎麦

Okay, let's talk soba for a quick minute. Soba noodles are made from hardy buckwheat, which is grown in areas not suitable for rice cultivation, like the breathtaking, mountainous Nagano Prefecture, deep in the Japanese Alps, which still produces the largest harvest of this grain. Soba noodles go way, way back to the twelfth century and became a popular fast food in Edo (today's Tokyo) starting in the 1600s. They're delicious, nutritious, and deeply ingrained in Japanese culture. In fact, Japanese people traditionally slurp down soba on New Year's Eve (*toshikoshi soba*) as a symbol of longevity (a nod to the hardy buckwheat plant's resilience and ability to withstand harsh mountainous winters). There are many types of soba, from all-buckwheat varieties to noodles cut with wheat (an 80/20 ratio is popular) for greater pliability—as all-buckwheat can be brittle. Which to choose? Try 'em and see what you like. Soba is enjoyed hot or cold, with a dipping sauce or in a broth. Here we share an all-vegetarian version that's super easy to prepare and loaded with mushroomy flavor that we love and know you will, too. The recipe calls for a trio of earthy Japanese mushrooms, but if you can't find one or two of the varieties, don't sweat it—just adjust the quantities, or mix and match (or substitute) with oyster or crimini mushrooms.

SERVES 4

½ cup fresh shiitake mushrooms

1 (4-ounce) package maitake mushrooms

1 (4-ounce) package shimeji mushrooms

6 cups Shiitake Dashi (page 43)

½ cup mirin

½ cup soy sauce

1 tablespoon potato starch (katakuriko)

12 ounces dried soba noodles (4 portions, see page 83)

¼ cup thinly sliced scallions

Shichimi togarashi

Prepare the mushrooms. Stem and slice the shiitake mushrooms. For the maitake, simply break them apart with your hands into small, bite-size clusters—no knife needed. For the shimeji, cut off and discard the base, then gently separate into small clusters with your hands.

Bring a large pot of water to a boil over medium-high heat to cook the soba.

In a large saucepan, bring the dashi, mirin, and soy sauce to a boil over medium-high heat. Once boiling, add all the mushrooms and reduce the heat to low to maintain a gentle simmer. Cook for about 2 minutes, until the mushrooms are just tender but still have some texture. Skim off any scum that appears on the surface.

While the mushrooms are cooking, create a slurry by mixing the potato starch with 1 tablespoon of water in a small bowl.

HOW TO BUY DRY SOBA

Perusing soba online or at your local H-Mart can be a head-scratcher. Too many choices, most of them with packaging in Japanese. Look for just four ingredients—buckwheat flour, wheat flour, water, and salt. That's it. A little wheat makes the noodles more elastic. Some soba omits the wheat—that's fine too. Try a brand or two and find your go-to. Soba often comes bundled into individual portions with little bands, each weighing about 3 ounces, a nice touch.

Slowly stir the slurry into the mushroom broth and keep stirring gently for 1 minute more, until the broth starts to thicken slightly—the potato starch will give the broth just the right amount of body. Cook the soba noodles in the pot of boiling water according to the package instructions. The noodles should retain a slight firmness when done, so be careful not to overcook them.

Divide the soba among four bowls, ladle the hot mushroom broth and mushrooms over the noodles. Top each bowl with the scallions and a sprinkling of shichimi togarashi. Serve immediately.

GOMA DARE SOBA

(COLD SESAME SOBA)

胡麻だれ蕎麦

This is your summer go-to noodle. We love cold soba. Slurping up these nutty, toothsome buckwheat noodles is pure joy. Hey, they've been keeping the Japanese cool for centuries, as Tadashi can attest—soba powered him through sweltering Augusts growing up in Tokyo, sans AC. Paired with a rich, refreshing sesame broth, fresh summer vegetables, crisp slivers of nori, and a pop of wasabi, this completely vegetarian soba will leave you happy, we promise. Other veggies—like blanched and cooled wax beans, green beans, or sugar snap peas—are also great in this recipe. There's enough broth here for leftovers, so you can keep cool all week. Finally, this recipe works wonderfully with somen, ramen, or udon noodles, too, if you want a little change-up for the next batch.

SERVES 4

SESAME BROTH

1¾ cups Shiitake Dashi (page 43)

½ cup Japanese sesame paste (neri goma)

½ cup rice vinegar

½ cup mirin

2 cups soy sauce

½ cup sugar

4 cups soy milk

12 ounces dried soba noodles (4 portions, see page 83)

1 medium cucumber (about 4 ounces), cut into thin strips

½ bunch asparagus (about 4 ounces), peeled, blanched, cooled, and cut into 2-inch lengths

1 medium avocado, sliced

½ small red onion (about 2 ounces), thinly sliced and soaked in cold water

2 teaspoons wasabi

Kizami (needle-cut) nori seaweed for garnish

Make the sesame broth. In a large bowl, whisk together the dashi, sesame paste, rice vinegar, mirin, soy sauce, sugar, and soy milk until smooth. (Depending on the package, you might need to knead the sesame paste a bit to get it all out.) Keep the broth in the refrigerator until you're ready to serve.

To cook the soba, first prepare an ice water bath in a large bowl and set it in the sink. Bring a large pot of water to a boil over high heat. Add the soba and cook for about 3 minutes, or until it is cooked through but still retains some bite. Drain and dunk the noodles in the ice water bath. When the noodles are cool, drain them and set aside.

Divide the soba among four serving bowls. Pour about 1 cup of the sesame broth over the noodles in each bowl. Top each bowl with equal portions of cucumber, asparagus, avocado, and drained red onion, arranging them in separate mounds. Add a small dab (about ½ teaspoon) of wasabi to each bowl. Sprinkle the kizami nori over the top for garnish.

Serve immediately, encouraging everyone to mix everything together before diving in. Refrigerate leftover broth for up to a week to use again.

KIMCHI RAMEN

キムチラーメン

Kimchi symbolizes Korea's identity and culture, and the popularity of these fiery fermented vegetables has spread across the globe. In Japan, cooks of all stripes put the naturally preserved, cabbage-and-chile version to work in a multitude of dishes. Perhaps the best known is this one, kimchi ramen, which can be enjoyed hot or cold. Here we opt to pair kimchi with a cold broth and springy noodles to create the perfect summer dish—cool, spicy, refreshing, and intensely satisfying. Slices of buta kakuni (braised pork belly, see page 239) and soft-boiled egg add heft, but if you don't have 'em, go without; you'll still love these noodles. For a vegetarian version, use an all-vegetarian kimchi (without the fish sauce and shrimp paste), omit the pork, and use vegetable stock instead of chicken stock. And feel free to adjust the amount of kimchi to your taste. If you like it spicier, add more kimchi and juice from the jar, or even a dollop of *gochujang* (Korean red chili paste) for extra heat. You'll also find a variation for hot kimchi ramen at the end of the recipe.

SERVES 4

Pinch of salt

2 eggs

BROTH

4 cups chicken stock (preferably no-sodium, or use homemade, see page 206)

¼ cup mirin

1 teaspoon salt

1 tablespoon usukuchi soy sauce

1 teaspoon toasted sesame oil

4 (4-ounce) servings fresh or frozen ramen noodles

⅔ pound kimchi, cut into bite-size pieces, plus kimchi juice from the jar

4 pieces Buta Kakuni (page 239), at room temperature, each piece cut in half lengthwise

¼ cup thinly sliced scallions

Prepare the soft-boiled eggs. Fill a small saucepan with water and a generous pinch of salt and bring to a boil over medium-high heat. Carefully add the eggs and cook for exactly 7 minutes. Transfer the saucepan to the sink. Pour off the boiling water and fill with cold running water to stop the cooking. As soon as the eggs are cool enough to handle, peel them and set aside.

Make the broth. Prepare an ice bath in a large bowl. In a medium saucepan, combine the chicken stock, mirin, salt, and usukuchi soy sauce. Bring the mixture to a boil over medium-high heat, then immediately remove from the heat. Stir in the sesame oil. Transfer the broth to a bowl and chill in the ice bath until cold, 15 to 20 minutes. (You can also make this ahead of time and chill in the refrigerator overnight.)

CONTINUED →

KIMCHI RAMEN, CONTINUED

While the broth is chilling, prepare the ramen noodles according to the package instructions, stirring occasionally to prevent clumping. Fresh noodles will only take 1 to 2 minutes, while dried may take 3 to 4 minutes. The noodles should retain their springiness (taste them!), so be careful not to overcook them. Drain the noodles in a colander and rinse under cold running water until completely cooled. Gently toss the noodles as you rinse to ensure they're chilled throughout.

As soon as the noodles are chilled, divide them among four large bowls—you don't want them to sit around for too long or they'll stick together. Pour the cold broth over the noodles and gently mix together, using chopsticks (ideal) or tongs to fold the noodles over—again, so the noodles don't clump. Spoon in a bit of the kimchi juice from the kimchi jar. Top each bowl with a generous portion of kimchi, slices of buta kakuni, and ½ soft-boiled egg. Scatter sliced scallions over the top and serve immediately.

P.S. If you have leftover roast chicken from our amazing soy-brined roast chicken recipe (see page 205), you can use it here in place of the buta kakuni. The cold chicken works beautifully in this dish.

VARIATION

To serve this ramen hot, simply heat up the broth and skip rinsing the noodles in cold water. Just divide the noodles among four bowls as soon as they're ready, pour the hot broth over them, and follow the rest of the recipe.

VEGGIE CURRY RAMEN

野菜カレーラーメン

For those of you who read our last book, *Japanese Soul Cooking* (available where all books are sold, hint, hint), you'll know that curry arrived in Japan in the late nineteenth century via the British navy, who themselves adopted it from Indian recipes, modifying the flavor and texture to suit their imperial tastes and creating a hearty veggie and meat dish to sustain seafaring sailors. Once this dish hit Japanese shores, it quickly became beloved and evolved further to suit local tastes, including as *kaigun* curry (Japan's own navy curry, still served on warships to this day) and beyond. This ramen version is a beautiful example: all-veggie, all-amazing. For this dish we employ summer vegetables, but since it's such an incredibly flexible recipe, don't sweat the exact veggies we call for—use any combination you want or have around. It's all good, you just want to add about 1½ pounds of vegetables total. In winter, for example, use root vegetables like sweet potato, carrots, onions, or burdock root, and maybe cabbage (white, red, napa, or Savoy). In autumn, try adding butternut, acorn, or kabocha squash. Cook the roots and squash longer, until they're tender, 10 to 15 minutes after you add the liquids (taste to test). The long and short: Play around and have fun with the recipe! (Isn't that what cooking's all about?) Also, if you're making this in the colder months, try swapping out the soy sauce for 2 tablespoons red miso and the olive oil for roasted sesame oil, giving the dish a heartier flavor profile to stand up to the roots. Whichever veggies you end up tossing into the pot, you'll love this ramen.

SERVES 4

¼ cup sake

3 tablespoons mirin

4 cups vegetable stock

3 tablespoons soy sauce

2 tablespoons olive oil

1 small onion, sliced

1 tablespoon sliced garlic

1 tablespoon finely chopped ginger

1 small lotus root, peeled, cut in half lengthwise, and sliced into ¼-inch-thick half-moons (keep it in water until ready to use)

1 small zucchini or yellow summer squash, cut into ½-inch slices

In a large bowl, combine the sake, mirin, vegetable stock, and soy sauce. Set aside.

In a large heavy-bottomed pot (preferably a Dutch oven), heat the olive oil over medium heat. Add the onion and cook for about 1 minute until it begins to soften. Add the garlic and ginger and cook for 2 minutes, stirring frequently. The aromatics should become fragrant.

Drain the lotus root, pat dry, and add to the pot. Cook for 2 minutes more, stirring frequently. Add the zucchini and cook for 1 minute, stirring constantly. Add the eggplant and cook for another minute, then add the red bell pepper and cook for 1 more minute.

CONTINUED →

S&B
ORIENTAL
CURRY

VEGGIE CURRY RAMEN, CONTINUED

1 small Japanese or Chinese eggplant, cut into ½-inch slices

1 small red bell pepper, thickly sliced

4 tablespoons Japanese curry powder (we like S&B brand)

1 medium tomato, chopped into big chunks

4 (4-ounce) packages fresh or frozen ramen noodles, preferably the thick Sapporo variety (or use thick, flat Chinese wonton noodles)

2 tablespoons sliced scallion

Sprinkle 3 tablespoons of curry powder over the vegetables. Stir to coat, then and cook for about 1 minute to toast the curry powder and release its fragrance.

Pour in the liquid. Bring to a boil, then reduce the heat and simmer for about 5 minutes, until the vegetables are tender but still have some bite. Add the remaining 1 tablespoon curry powder and the chopped tomato to the simmering curry. Cook for an additional 2 minutes until the tomatoes are just heated through.

While the curry simmers, cook the ramen noodles according to package instructions, stirring occasionally to prevent clumping. Fresh noodles will take only 1 to 2 minutes, while dried may take 3 to 4 minutes (taste them!). The noodles should retain their springiness, so be careful not to overcook them.

Drain the noodles and divide them among four bowls. (Don't rinse them—you want the noodles hot.) Ladle the hot curry vegetable mixture over the noodles and garnish with sliced scallions. Enjoy immediately while the noodles are still springy and the broth is hot.

TORi POTA RAMEN
(CHICKEN "POTAGE" RAMEN)
鶏ポタラーメン

We love, love, love ramen. (We even teamed up to run a popular ramen joint in Brooklyn back in the 2010s.) We think this up-and-coming style is fantastic, and totally achievable at home, so here we go. Tori pota is an updated version of tori paitan, a hearty chicken ramen associated with the Osaka area. *Paitan* literally means "white soup" in Japanese, and that's what you get—a creamy, cloudy soup (ramen broth, by the way, is called "soup," even in Japan). *Pota* is short for "potage," which in French cooking refers to a traditional thick soup or stew. Pota has been adopted in Japan to mean a more contemporary ramen that's lighter than traditional *paitan* (also sometimes referred to as "potage"). Go figure. Okay, that's it for etymology class. This recipe is inspired by one Chef Yoshiteru Ikegawa, a.k.a. Japan's top yakitori chef, who serves potage at his restaurants in Tokyo. The velvety soup here is layered with irresistible flavors, including fiery yuzu kosho, which contributes a satisfying kick. The steamed chicken is so tender and beautiful we use it in another dish inspired by Mr. Ikegawa's cooking (see page 202). Thanks, Chef! Now, remember your ramen etiquette: Eat it piping hot. Eat it quickly. And slurp your noodles, for God's sake! Loudly! Not only does this action cool the noodles as they barrel toward your gullet, but it helps aerate the soup, which enhances the taste and aroma of the ramen. Get cracking and go to town.

SERVES 4

STEAMED CHICKEN

2 (6-ounce) boneless, skinless chicken breasts

½ teaspoon salt

1 teaspoon sliced ginger

2 tablespoons sake

SOUP

6 cups chicken stock (preferably low- or no-sodium, or use homemade, see page 206)

¼ cup sake

1 teaspoon rice vinegar

¼ cup sliced white onion

1 tablespoon sliced garlic

½ tablespoon sliced ginger

1 tablespoon rice flour

1 teaspoon red yuzu kosho

2 teaspoons salt, plus more as needed

4 portions ramen noodles (fresh or dried)

Prepare the chicken. In a small saucepan that can fit the chicken breasts snugly, add the chicken, salt, ginger, and sake. (The aromatics will infuse the chicken as it cooks.) Bring to a boil over high heat, then cover, reduce the heat to low, and simmer for 3 minutes. Flip the chicken, cover, and simmer for 2 more minutes. Turn off the heat and let sit, still covered, for 15 minutes (it'll be just-cooked and ready to eat!). The residual heat will gently cook the chicken through, resulting in super tender, juicy meat. Once done, remove the chicken, slice it against the grain, and set aside. Reserve the steaming liquid for the soup.

Make the soup. In a large pot, bring the chicken stock, sake, rice vinegar, onion, garlic, and ginger to a boil over medium heat, then reduce the heat to low and let it simmer gently for about 10 minutes, allowing the flavors to meld and the vegetables to soften.

CONTINUED →

TORi POTA RAMEN, CONTINUED

TOPPINGS

1 cup chopped green or Savoy cabbage, cut into 1-inch squares

2 eggs

¼ cup sliced bamboo shoots (use canned or packaged precooked bamboo shoots, optional)

¼ cup thinly sliced scallions

While the soup is simmering, prepare the toppings. Prepare an ice bath in a large bowl, then bring a pot of water to a boil and blanch the cabbage for 1 to 2 minutes until it's bright green and slightly tender. Immediately transfer the cabbage to the ice bath to stop the cooking, then drain into a colander and cool under cold running water. Squeeze out as much excess water as you can with your hands and set aside.

For the eggs, bring another pot of water to a boil, gently lower the eggs into the water, and cook for exactly 7 minutes for a perfectly soft-boiled center. Optional step: For the first minute of cooking, use a spoon to gently roll the eggs around in the pot so the yolks set in the center, making the eggs even more beautiful. Transfer the eggs to a bowl filled with cold water, peel when cool enough to handle, and set aside.

Once the soup has simmered for 10 minutes, add the rice flour, which will thicken the soup and give it body and its signature white hue. Whisk well to ensure there are no lumps. Add the reserved chicken steaming liquid. Increase the heat to medium, bring the soup to a boil, and cook for about 1 minute, until the broth starts to thicken slightly.

Now carefully transfer the hot broth to a blender. Blend in batches: Secure the lid tightly, covering it with a kitchen towel for extra precaution, as hot liquids can expand when blended. Blend on low speed and gradually increase it to high (for safety, since hot broth could explode out of the blender if you start on high) for about 30 seconds until the broth becomes smooth and emulsified. Return the blended soup to the pot and keep warm over low heat. Stir in the yuzu kosho, and add salt to taste.

In a separate pot of boiling water, cook the ramen noodles according to the package instructions, stirring occasionally to prevent clumping. Fresh noodles will take only 1 to 2 minutes, while dried may take 3 to 4 minutes (taste them!). The noodles should retain their springiness, so be careful not to overcook them.

Drain the noodles and divide them among four bowls. (Don't rinse them; you want the noodles hot.) Ladle the hot, creamy soup over the noodles. Top each bowl with a portion of the sliced chicken (room temperature is fine), blanched cabbage, and half a soft-boiled egg, arranging the ingredients neatly. Add the bamboo shoots, if using. Finish with a sprinkle of sliced scallions and serve immediately, piping hot.

P.S. This ramen also works great with somen noodles.

KAMA-AGE UDON

釜あげうどん

Possibly the ultimate midnight snack. Or a speedy lunch. Or a go-to any time you're hankering for a dish that's quick and dirty and so incredibly satisfying. *Kama-age* ("kama-ageh") literally means "lifted from the pot," and honestly, there's not much more to this dish than that. Originating sometime in the 1600–1700s, this was fast food for the working class: fat, chewy udon noodles tossed with a rich, silky raw egg yolk that acts as a sauce, amped up with aromatic roasted sesame oil and umami-fueled tamari soy sauce. Add a sprinkle of scallions, and that's basically it. (If you want to flavor this dish some more, sprinkle shichimi togarashi over it or add a dab of yuzu kosho.) Use super fresh eggs from the farmers' market or your chickens out back, if you're lucky to have some. And if raw yolk isn't your jam, cook onsen tamago or poached eggs (see page 96) for this dish—also beautiful.

SERVES 4

4 (4-ounce) packages frozen cooked udon

4 fresh, raw egg yolks, or Onsen Tamago (page 96)

4 tablespoons tamari soy sauce

2 teaspoons toasted sesame oil

¼ cup sliced scallions

Bring a large pot of water to a boil and add the frozen udon noodles. Reheat the udon until the water comes back to a boil, 1 to 2 minutes. The noodles should be heated through but still chewy.

Immediately drain the noodles and divide them among four serving bowls.

Top each bowl with an egg yolk or onsen egg. Drizzle each serving with 1 tablespoon tamari soy sauce and ½ teaspoon sesame oil. Garnish with sliced scallions and serve immediately, instructing everyone to mix everything with the noodles before digging in.

EGGS TWO WAYS

Onsen Tamago

These eggs, literally "hot spring eggs," have been cooked in Japan's bountiful hot springs (*onsen*) since at least the eighth century, if not earlier. At the onsen, eggs are simply dunked into the hot spring water for a spell to create a unique texture—silky whites and a custard-like yolk, the result of the whites and yolks solidifying at different points (thanks to the precise temperature of hot springs). To achieve this effect at home, bring 4 cups water to a boil in a saucepan. Remove from the heat and add 1 cup cold water to get the water temperature down to 170°F (use a thermometer; this temperature is key). Now add 4 eggs and let them sit, covered, for 10 minutes. Remove the eggs and carefully crack into each bowl of udon.

Poached Eggs

Alternatively, you can cook classic poached eggs (also great with Tamago Kake Gohan, page 63). Here's the foolproof method: Prepare a bowl with cold water. In a small saucepan over medium-high heat, bring 4 cups water and 1 tablespoon white vinegar to a boil. As soon as it boils, reduce the heat to a simmer. Cook 1 egg at a time: Crack 1 egg into a small bowl and gently swirl the water with chopsticks or a spoon before sliding the egg into the middle of the saucepan (the swirling will keep the egg whites together instead of spreading out when they hit the water; you want a nice, tight poached egg). Cook for 1 to 2 minutes until the whites have solidified around the yolk. Remove the egg with a slotted spoon and transfer it to the bowl with cold water to stop the cooking. Repeat with the other eggs.

NAGOYA KiSHiMEN

(NAGOYA-STYLE CHICKEN AND MISO NOODLES)

名古屋きしめん

These noodles trace their origin back hundreds of years and are a cornerstone of the cuisine of Nagoya City, hence the name. Kishimen are flat, ribbon-like wheat noodles that are wider and thinner than udon, Japan's classic wheat noodle. They have a lovely soft but chewy texture and are typically served in both hot and cold broths. Here we share a satisfying, hearty hot broth powered by bold, intensely flavored hatcho miso (see page 98) and fortified with chicken—two other ingredients central to Nagoya's culinary identity. (Nagoya even boasts its own breed of heirloom chicken, the Nagoya Cochin.) These noodles are super good, easy to prepare, and perfect for a blustery day. You can find kishimen in Japanese markets. In a pinch, substitute with udon noodles.

SERVES 4

- 2 pieces abura age (fried tofu)
- Boiling water, for rinsing the abura
- ¼ pound burdock root
- 1½ teaspoons sesame oil
- ½ cup thinly sliced carrots (cut on the diagonal)
- 1 pound boneless, skinless chicken breast, thinly sliced
- ½ cup fresh shiitake mushrooms (4 or 5 mushrooms), stemmed and thinly sliced
- 2 tablespoons mirin
- 1 tablespoon sake
- 6 cups dashi (see page 40)
- ¾ cup hatcho miso
- 1 package kishimen noodles (about 9.5 ounces)
- 2 tablespoons chopped scallions (optional)
- Shichimi togarashi (optional)
- Sansho (optional)

Place the abura age pieces in a colander in the sink. Pour boiling water over them to remove excess oil on both sides. Use chopsticks to press out excess water and let sit until cool to the touch. Slice the abura age into thin strips and set aside.

Under cold running water, use steel wool or a scrubby to gently rub off the brown exterior of the burdock root until you see the pale white flesh (it doesn't have to be perfect). Thinly slice crosswise and keep in water until ready to use to prevent discoloration (you should have about ½ cup sliced burdock).

In a large heavy-bottomed pot (preferably a Dutch oven), heat the sesame oil over medium heat. Drain the burdock root and add it to the pot. Cook, stirring frequently, for about 2 minutes, until it starts to look glossy. Add the carrots and cook for another minute, stirring frequently. Add the chicken and cook until it begins to turn white but isn't fully cooked, about 2 minutes, using chopsticks or tongs to separate any pieces that stick together. Add the shiitake mushrooms and continue cooking for another 1 minute.

Add the mirin and sake, letting them simmer for 30 seconds to cook off the alcohol. Add the dashi and bring to a boil. Reduce the heat to medium and let simmer for about 5 minutes, until

CONTINUED →

the chicken is cooked through and the vegetables are tender but still have some bite. Skim off any foam that rises to the surface with a fine-mesh skimmer or spoon.

While the soup simmers, place the hatcho miso in a fine-mesh strainer and lower it into the pot so it's partially submerged in the hot broth. Using the back of a spoon or a wooden spatula, gradually push the miso through the strainer while stirring it into the broth. Once all the miso is dissolved, reduce the heat to low; this gentle heat preserves the miso's flavor.

Add the abura age and simmer gently for another minute to heat through. Keep the soup on a low simmer until the noodles are ready.

In a separate pot of boiling water, cook the kishimen noodles according to the package instructions, stirring occasionally to prevent clumping. The noodles should be cooked through and tender but still chewy, 4 to 5 minutes. Taste them and watch carefully so you don't overcook.

Drain the noodles and divide them among four bowls. (Don't rinse them; you want the noodles hot.) Ladle the hot soup over the noodles, making sure each bowl gets an equal portion of chicken, vegetables, and abura age. If you'd like, garnish with the scallions, and shichimi togarashi or sansho (or both). Serve immediately while piping hot.

P.S. The soup base (without noodles) can be made a day ahead and gently reheated. Just cook the noodles fresh when ready to serve.

HATCHO MISO

Hatcho is one of our absolute favorite misos that's been produced continuously for more than eight hundred years on a very specific street, eight blocks (*hatcho* means "eight") from a particular castle near the city of Nagoya. Only two of these producers remain today. So what makes this miso so magnificent? It's produced from just two ingredients—soybeans and salt. With just these ingredients, miso fermentation can begin only when enough weight is added to create the necessary pressure to trigger the chemical transformation. So to produce this miso, three tons of massive river stones, arranged like pyramids, press down on huge cedar vats the size of small cars filled with steamed soybeans and salt. It's quite a sight! Fermentation lasts for about three years and results in a deep ruddy-brown, super dense, intense miso with a powerful, complex flavor that offers hints of bitterness and astringency. If you can't find hatcho, substitute with a nice aka miso, which is made from soybeans, rice, and salt and fermented for at least a couple of years. Aka miso is easy to find, and also amazing.

4

SALADS AND VEGETARIAN SOZAI

サラダ、惣菜

As we discuss in the book's introduction, a Japanese meal isn't simply a procession of courses: appetizer, main course, dessert. It's a play of dishes featuring a combo of ingredients, textures, cooking methods, and colors, the sum of which yields delicious, fun, and intrinsically healthy eating without having to overthink it.

But how to knock out a bunch of dishes every time you sit for dinner? That's where the recipes in this chapter come in. The salads and *sozai* (we'll get to that in a minute) we share are easy and versatile and can be kept at the ready in the fridge to quickly fill out a meal.

Let's start with salad. Fresh leafy greens and other veggies tossed with dressing are a recent addition to Japanese cuisine. Historically, raw vegetables in Japan were more likely to appear as simple *tsukemono* (pickles) or as garnishes. In the last few decades, though, the Japanese have adopted Western salads—and adapted them, too. We'll share a bunch of salads with delicious dressings you can whip up in a snap and keep in the fridge to use again and again.

Sozai refers to homey side dishes. There are a wide variety of them; here we focus on all-vegetarian examples. If you live in Japan, you can find ready-made sozai at your local department store *depachika,* supermarket, or even *konbini,* the ubiquitous convenience stores (see page 103). If, like us, you don't live in Japan, you can easily prepare the dishes ahead of time and reap the benefits of leftovers. Let's get started.

FOOD SHOPPING: DEPACHIKA AND KONBINI

Among the many wonderful things about living in Japan is this: Your local *depachika* stands ready with high-quality ingredients and freshly prepared dishes for you to buy and feast on at home. Depachika are food markets found in every department store. They're always located in the basement (*depa* for "department store" and *chika* for "basement"), sometimes even plunging two or three levels deep. And they're always packed with incredible offerings.

Depachika got their start about ninety years ago in the city of Nagoya, where the Matsuzakaya department store created in its basement a "street of specialty stores" focused on food. The idea caught on and soon other department stores across the country followed suit. Today, some depachika feature up to thirty thousand products in a single department store, from beautiful sushi, French pastries, and fine chocolates to beckoning platters of freshly made sozai, tempura, onigiri, and rows and rows of pristine vegetables, fish, and meat. More than just a giant market, depachika are a testament to a mind-blowing food culture, one that honors the country's passion for quality ingredients, presentation, and service. Make sure to check out a depachika when you visit Japan! (We love the massive depachika at Takashimaya's flagship store, a short walk from Tokyo Station.)

Like depachika, *konbini* are a fixture of Japanese food culture (and life)—but by an order of magnitude greater. *Konbini* are simply convenience stores. But they ain't nothing like your local 7-Eleven. Since their introduction in the mid-1970s, konbini like Lawson, Natural Lawson, FamilyMart (famous for its *Famichiki* fried chicken), and, yes, 7-Eleven (which is actually Japanese-owned) dot every city, town, village, and hamlet in Japan. There are more than 55,000 of them in a country with roughly the same square mileage as Montana. (And if that stat isn't impressive enough, by comparison the *entire* United States has 152,000 convenience stores.)

What makes konbini special? At these convenience stores, you'll find household items, yes, but also fresh, high-quality prepared meals that rival restaurant fare. In fact, it was the introduction of tasty onigiri rice balls in 1978 at Japanese 7-Elevens that supercharged their growth across the country. Today, konbini offer bento boxes, sozai, sandwiches, regional cooking, coffee-house-level coffee and more—these stores introduce more than a hundred new items each month with big red stickers announcing "now on sale." And even their humble onigiri now boasts premium *Koshihikari* rice. Remember, people, we're talking about *convenience stores*.

And more than amazing food, konbini serve as neighborhood hubs where you can pull cash out of ATMs; make copies; pay bills; buy socks, dress shirts, and ties (for a quick presto-chango after an unfortunate yakitori incident); surf free Wi-Fi; and on and on, twenty-four hours a day.

Don't you wish we had these here? (Are you listening, corporate 7-Eleven?)

FIVE SALADS

サラダ五種

The following salads feature a blend of Western and Eastern ingredients and flavors, with dressings involving miso, wasabi, toasted sesame oil, soy sauce, and more. They're a delight and exemplify the Japanese adaptation of salads. But beyond our recipes . . . well, you already know how to make a salad. So go ahead and try the dressings with different components or fewer components, and come up with something new, too!

AVOCADO-ARUGULA SALAD WITH SESAME-SCALLION DRESSING

アヴォカドとアルグラのサラダ

Consider this our "all-purpose" *wafu* salad dressing (*wafu* means "Japanese-style"). It's super versatile and can last up to a week, so keep a jar of it in the fridge for a quick weeknight salad. Vary the salad ingredients, too, and for another dressing variation, sub the scallions with 2 tablespoons of finely chopped scallions.

SERVES 4

DRESSING

¼ cup finely chopped scallions

¼ cup rice vinegar

3 tablespoons soy sauce

2 tablespoons mirin

2 tablespoons sesame oil

2 teaspoons freshly grated ginger

1 teaspoon sugar

SALAD

½ cup asparagus (5 stalks), cut into 1-inch pieces

4 cups packed arugula

1 ripe avocado, cut into ½-inch cubes

1 small Persian cucumber, unpeeled and thinly sliced into coins

3 red radishes, thinly sliced

¼ medium red onion, thinly sliced

2 teaspoons sesame seeds

Make the dressing. Combine all dressing ingredients in a bowl and whisk until well blended. Set aside to let the flavors meld.

Fill a bowl with cold water and set aside. Bring a small pot of salted water to a boil over high heat and add the asparagus. Cook for 1 to 2 minutes until the asparagus is bright green and tender-crisp. Be careful not to overcook. Immediately transfer the asparagus to the bowl to stop the cooking. Once cooled, drain and pat dry.

Make the salad. In a large bowl, combine the arugula, avocado, cucumber, asparagus, radish, and red onion. Just before serving, drizzle the salad with the sesame-scallion dressing and toss gently to coat. Be careful not to overmix, as the avocado can become mushy.

Divide the salad among four plates, or use a serving bowl for sharing. Garnish with a sprinkle of toasted sesame seeds and serve immediately.

SHREDDED CABBAGE WITH CREAMY DAIKON DRESSING

キャベツ千切りと大根ドレッシング

This easy-peasy salad pairs wonderfully with rich fried foods, acting as a refreshing counterpoint. And daikon helps the body absorb oily foods, so it's both delicious and good for you.

SERVES 4

DAIKON DRESSING

¼ pound daikon radish, roughly chopped

¼ cup rice vinegar

2 tablespoons chopped white onion

2 tablespoons extra-virgin olive oil

1 tablespoon wasabi paste

1 tablespoon sugar

1 teaspoon salt

SALAD

4 cups finely sliced white or red cabbage (see Note)

1 small carrot, thinly sliced into coins

Make the dressing. Combine all the dressing ingredients in a blender. Blend for 1 to 2 minutes until smooth and creamy. The dressing should have a balance of tangy, sweet, and wasabi-spicy flavors with a smooth, pourable consistency. Set aside.

Make the salad. Place the sliced cabbage in a large bowl filled with cold water. Let it soak for about 5 minutes to crisp the cabbage. Drain well and pat dry with a clean kitchen towel or paper towels.

In a large bowl, combine the cabbage and carrot and add about ¾ cup of the daikon dressing. Toss gently but thoroughly to ensure the vegetables are evenly coated.

Divide the salad among four plates, or use a serving bowl for sharing. Drizzle a little extra dressing on top if you'd like. The salad is best enjoyed immediately, while the cabbage is at its crispest.

NOTE

Prepare the cabbage by first slicing it in half (tip to tail) and cutting out the core. Separate the leaves from each half and cut out any thick ribs, then stack and slice into thin strips. This methodical preparation is important for achieving the right texture.

KALE SALAD WITH SESAME DRESSING

ケールサラダと胡麻ドレッシング

Like the dressing in the Spinach-Fennel Salad (page 109), dashi delivers a delicious dose of umami here. Use your dashi cubes!

SERVES 4

SESAME DRESSING

¼ cup toasted sesame seeds

¼ cup Shiitake Dashi (page 43)

2 tablespoons rice vinegar

2 tablespoons usukuchi soy sauce

1 tablespoon sugar

¼ teaspoon ground white pepper

Pinch of salt

SALAD

¼ cup carrot ribbons (use a vegetable peeler)

½ cup green beans, trimmed

4 cups kale, cut into bite-size pieces

2 teaspoons black sesame seeds (white is fine, too)

Make the dressing. Combine the dressing ingredients in a blender. Blend for 1 to 2 minutes until smooth and well combined. The dressing should have a runny, creamy consistency with a rich, nutty flavor. Set aside.

Make the salad. Place the carrot ribbons in a bowl of cold water and let them soak for about 5 minutes. This will help them become crisp and slightly curled. Drain and pat dry.

Fill a medium bowl halfway with cold water. Bring a pot of salted water to a boil. Add the green beans and cook for 2 to 3 minutes until they're bright green and tender-crisp. Be careful not to overcook. Immediately transfer the green beans to the bowl to stop the cooking. Once cooled, drain, pat dry, and cut into about 1-inch pieces.

In a large bowl, add the kale and massage gently with your hands for 1 to 2 minutes to soften the leaves and make them more tender.

Add the carrot ribbons and green beans to the bowl with the kale. Drizzle the sesame dressing over the vegetables. Toss gently but thoroughly to ensure all the vegetables are well coated.

Divide the salad among four plates, or use a serving bowl for sharing. Sprinkle with the sesame seeds for garnish. Serve immediately.

HEIRLOOM TOMATOES AND TOFU WITH SHISO DRESSING

トマトと豆腐のサラダ紫蘇ドレッシング

This is the quintessential summer salad, when beautiful tomatoes and shiso are in peak season, or *shun,* as it's known in Japanese (see page 120).

SERVES 4

SALAD

¼ cup thinly sliced red onion

1 pound vine-ripened heirloom tomatoes, cut into 1-inch cubes

2 small Persian cucumbers, cut into 1-inch cubes

Salt

1 (14-ounce) package firm tofu, drained, patted dry, and cut into 1-inch cubes

SHISO DRESSING

½ cup extra-virgin olive oil

¼ cup packed shiso leaves, stems trimmed

2 tablespoons shiro miso (see page 20)

1 tablespoon sugar

1 teaspoon green yuzu kosho

1 garlic clove, roughly chopped

Prepare the onion. In a small bowl, combine the red onion slices with enough cold water to cover and let soak for about 10 minutes. This will help remove some of the harshness but keep the lovely oniony flavor. After soaking, drain and pat dry.

Make the dressing. Combine the dressing ingredients in a blender. Blend for 1 to 2 minutes until smooth and vibrant green. Set aside.

Make the salad. In a large bowl, combine the tomatoes and cucumbers. Lightly season with salt and toss gently. Add the red onion and tofu to the bowl and gently fold in, being careful not to break apart the tofu.

Divide the salad among four bowls. Drizzle the shiso dressing generously over each serving, allowing it to coat the vegetables and tofu. Avoid tossing the salad with the dressing to maintain the integrity of the tofu and tomatoes.

Serve immediately, encouraging everyone to mix the dressing into their individual portions as they eat.

SPINACH-FENNEL SALAD WITH MISO DRESSING

法連草とフェンネルのサラダ味噌ドレッシング

Remember "dashi cubes," which we mention in the dashi recipes? Use 'em for this fantastic dressing to add umami goodness and cut the thickness of the miso.

SERVES 4

MISO DRESSING

¼ cup Shiitake Dashi (page 43)

2 tablespoons shiro miso (see page 20)

2 tablespoons rice vinegar

1 tablespoon sugar

1 tablespoon chopped scallions, white part only

1 tablespoon toasted sesame oil

1 teaspoon karashi mustard

SALAD

4 cups packed baby spinach

½ cup thinly sliced fennel

¼ cup cherry tomatoes, cut in half

¼ cup thinly sliced scallions, green part only

Make the dressing. Combine the dressing ingredients in a blender. Blend for about 1 minute until smooth and well combined. The dressing will be more runny than thick, but that's fine. Taste and adjust the seasoning if needed. The dressing should have a balance of savory, sweet, and tangy flavors with a smooth consistency. Set aside.

Make the salad. In a large bowl, add the baby spinach, fennel, and tomatoes. Toss gently to mix. Drizzle about half of the miso dressing over the salad and toss gently to coat the vegetables evenly. Add more dressing as needed, being careful not to overdress the salad.

Divide the salad among four plates, or use a serving bowl for sharing. Garnish with a sprinkle of the scallions and serve.

TWO MORE SALAD DRESSINGS!

Hey, we couldn't stop at just five. Here are a couple of more super simple salad dressings to add to your weekday meal playbook. They call for Japanese pantry ingredients that you'll want to have on hand, and they take, oh, under sixty seconds to whip up. The first is ponzu-based, which adds citrusy umami and acid to any salad: Whisk together 3 parts ponzu with 1 part extra-virgin olive oil. Buy or make ponzu ahead of time (read our note on ponzu on page 129). The second relies on sushi vinegar to add delicate sweetness and acid. This is another ingredient you can buy or make ahead of time (read more on page 150). Whisk together 1 part sushi vinegar with 1 part sesame oil and 1 part soy sauce for an aromatic and versatile dressing.

SOZAi
惣菜

The recipes that follow are classic examples of vegetarian sozai. You can serve them in big bowls for sharing, if you'd like. Kinpira, goma-ae, and hijiki can be made ahead of time and kept in the fridge for up to a week.

WAKAME SUNOMONO
わかめ酢の物

Wakame is a seaweed with a long history, and not just culinary. It has played a part in Shinto ceremonies for centuries and even served as currency to remit taxes during the Nara Period in the eighth century. Ah, to pay taxes with sea vegetables . . . A versatile dried ingredient found in many Japanese dishes, including the standard-issue miso soup at your local sushi joint, wakame is easy to prepare, delicious, and nutrient dense. In this recipe we prepare it as *sunomono*, literally "vinegared thing," a classic preparation centered on rice vinegar, which is less acidic and slightly sweeter than Western vinegars. The vinegar is balanced by sugar and soy sauce to create a beautiful, bright, tangy flavor profile. Here we marry wakame with cucumber, a traditional combination. Jazz up this recipe, if you'd like, with poached squid, shrimp, octopus, or scallops (mix in or throw on top). And you can also prepare sunomono with only thinly sliced cucumbers or thinly sliced carrots, daikon, beets, celery, cabbage, or even romaine lettuce. So versatile! Sunomono dishes pair particularly well with rich or fried foods, offering a fresh contrast to heavier dishes.

SERVES 4

3 tablespoons dried wakame

2 Persian cucumbers, sliced into coins as thinly as possible (about ½ cup)

Salt

2 tablespoons rice vinegar

1 tablespoon sugar

1 teaspoon soy sauce

1 teaspoon toasted white sesame seeds

1 tablespoon ginger, cut into thin needles called hari shoga (optional, see sidebar)

In a medium bowl, combine the dried wakame with enough cold water to cover. Let it soak for about 15 minutes, until it's fully reconstituted and tender. Drain the wakame in a colander and gently squeeze out any excess water. If the pieces are very large, roughly chop them for easier eating. Set aside.

CONTINUED →

WAKAME SUNOMONO, CONTINUED

While the wakame is soaking, prepare the cucumbers. Place the cucumbers in a bowl and sprinkle with ¼ teaspoon salt. Gently massage the salt into the cucumbers with your hands. Let them sit for about 15 minutes, to allow the salt to draw out excess moisture and season and cure the cucumbers.

Meanwhile, in a small bowl, whisk together the rice vinegar, sugar, and soy sauce until the sugar is fully dissolved.

When the cucumbers are ready, take handfuls of the cucumber slices and squeeze them firmly to remove as much liquid as possible. This step is crucial for achieving the right texture in your sunomono.

In a serving bowl, combine the drained wakame and squeezed cucumber slices. Pour the dressing over the vegetables and toss gently to coat evenly. Let the salad sit for a few minutes to allow the flavors to meld.

Sprinkle the salad with the toasted sesame seeds, top with the ginger, if you'd like, and serve immediately. You can also prepare this dish a few hours ahead of time refrigerate it, but the wakame is best the day it's made—it doesn't keep.

P.S. If you can't find Persian cucumbers, you can use any variety of cucumber. Just be sure to peel them and remove the seeds, as they can make the sunomono watery.

HARI SHOGA

Hari shoga is a cutting technique in which fresh ginger is sliced into thin, needle-like strips (*hari shoga* means "needle ginger"). Aside from adding a spicy, aromatic kick, ginger is used in Japanese cooking to neutralize the fishy smell that can be present in seafood, and seaweed for that matter. Cutting ginger hari shoga style takes a bit of practice—and a seriously sharp knife. Peel a knob of fresh ginger and slice it very thinly across the grain. Aim for paper-thin slices 1 to 2 millimeters thick—so thin we gotta go metric! Stack 3 or 4 of these slices on top of one another and cut the stack into very fine strips, as thin as you can manage. Repeat with the remaining ginger. Soak the needles in cold water for a few minutes to crisp them up and mellow the flavor. When you're ready to use, drain the ginger and gently squeeze out any excess water.

SPINACH OHITASHI

法蓮草お浸し

We talk a lot in this book about how dishes have adapted to modern cooking. But not ohitashi. Here no culinary evolution is necessary—why mess with perfection? Ohitashi is disarmingly simple: You blanch vegetables, then steep them in a seasoned dashi. This technique, which has been an integral part of Japanese cuisine for centuries, reflects its very essence, showcasing the importance of seasonal vegetables (especially vegetables in *shun*, or their peak flavor, see page 120), minimal preparation, and enhancing natural flavors with traditional seasonings. But while ohitashi is deep, it's also a beloved everyday staple that complements any dish on the dining table. For this recipe we use spinach, but ohitashi is also lovely with shungiku (chrysanthemum greens), asparagus, okra, broccoli, yu choy, bok choy, or even Swiss chard (a personal favorite of Tadashi's).

SERVES 4

1 pound spinach

2 cups dashi, or Shiitake Dashi (see page 43)

2 tablespoons mirin

3 tablespoons soy sauce

2 teaspoons sesame seeds

Prepare an ice water bath in a large bowl (or the sink). Bring a large pot of water to a boil over high heat. Add the spinach and blanch for about 30 seconds, until the leaves turn bright green and begin to soften. Immediately transfer the spinach to the ice water bath to stop the cooking and preserve its vibrant color. (If your spinach has large stems, place the stems in the boiling water first for about 60 seconds before dunking the leaves.)

Once cooled, drain the spinach thoroughly. Using your hands, squeeze out as much water as possible. This is a crucial step—the less water in the spinach, the better it will absorb the flavorful dashi without diluting it. Cut the spinach into roughly 2-inch lengths.

In a medium bowl, combine the dashi, mirin, and soy sauce. Add the squeezed spinach, making sure it's fully submerged. Allow the spinach to steep in the liquid for at least 30 minutes at room temperature. You'll see that the spinach absorbs much of the dashi mixture.

When you're ready to serve, gently squeeze the excess liquid from the spinach back into the bowl. You have two choices for serving: Arrange the spinach on a large serving platter and spoon a little of the dashi over the leaves or divide the spinach among four serving dishes, arranging it neatly, and spoon a little of the dashi mixture over each. Either way, garnish with the sesame seeds and serve.

You'll want to enjoy the ohitashi right away; it doesn't last in the refrigerator.

RENKON KINPIRA

蓮根きんぴら

Kintarō, a.k.a. Golden Boy, was a child with superhuman strength who, according to Japanese folklore, was raised by a mountain witch in the forests of Mount Ashigara. He became a fearless warrior and begat a son named Kinpira. Young Kinpira grew up to become powerful and brave like his dad, and *his* name came to represent strength and courage in Japanese culture. Ultimately, "Kinpira" evolved into the name for this dish, which is composed of root vegetables (a symbol of strength) and known for its nutritional value. Kinpira can be cooked with a variety of roots—often burdock but also carrots or carrots and burdock together or even non-Japanese roots like parsnips. Lotus root (*renkon*) is also a standard, and so crunchy and delicious that we made it the star of this recipe. But you can use this method for the other roots, too. Rather than slicing, though, shave burdock and carrots (and parsnips) like you're sharpening a pencil with a knife, if that image even resonates these days—if not, google it!

SERVES 4

1 pound lotus root

1 small dried Japanese red chile pepper

2 tablespoons sake

1 tablespoon sugar

2 tablespoons soy sauce

2 tablespoons water

1 tablespoon sesame oil

1 teaspoon toasted white sesame seeds

Peel the lotus root, slice it in half lengthwise, and cut into ¼-inch-thick half-moons. Immediately submerge the slices in cold water for 10 minutes; this prevents discoloration and removes excess starch, ensuring a crisper texture. Meanwhile, in a small bowl, soak the dried chile pepper in hot water for 10 minutes to soften, then remove the seeds and finely chop. (Sometimes you can find dried Japanese chiles presliced, so no soaking necessary; and if you can't find them, substitute ½ teaspoon red chile flakes.)

In a small bowl, whisk together the sake, sugar, soy sauce, and water. Set aside.

Drain the lotus root and pat dry thoroughly. Preheat a large cast-iron skillet (ideal) over medium heat. Pour in the sesame oil, then add the lotus root. Sauté for 3 minutes, stirring constantly. The lotus root will start to look glossy; searing it in oil firms up the surface a bit, which keeps it from breaking apart while cooking.

Add the sake mixture and the chopped chile to the skillet. Simmer over medium heat for 5 to 7 minutes, stirring frequently so each piece of lotus root is nicely coated. The fragrant, amazing liquid will reduce, forming a glossy coating. When the liquid has nearly evaporated and the lotus root is tender-crisp (taste it!), it's done.

Transfer to a serving dish and sprinkle with the sesame seeds. Serve hot, cold, or at room temp, all fantastic.

CAULIFLOWER GOMA-AE

カリフラワー胡麻和え

This dish is a perfect example of the evolution of Japanese cooking. *Goma-ae* means, roughly, "dressed with sesame sauce." Traditionally, vegetables that receive this treatment—like spinach, green beans, or broccoli—are blanched. And that's a tasty option. But by kicking it up a notch with the simple act of roasting (roasting veggies being more European), you're adding aromatic, caramelized cauliflower flavors to the nutty, sweet-and-savory dressing. Still a totally Japanese dish but also new and exciting and delicious. And easy, thanks to the suribachi! The suribachi is a Japanese mortar with a ridged pottery base that helps break down seeds and other small ingredients more effectively than a smooth mortar. We're not big into a million gadgets in the kitchen but this incredible tool is worth buying. Use it for any kind of mortar and pestling, and not just for Japanese cooking. Alternatively, you can use a regular mortar and pestle or even a spice or coffee grinder. The key is grinding sesame seeds fresh for this dish to release their showstopping fragrance.

SERVES 4

1 large head cauliflower (about 2 pounds), cut into 1-inch florets

½ teaspoon salt

2 tablespoons sesame oil

4 tablespoons toasted white sesame seeds

2 tablespoons soy sauce

1 teaspoon sugar

Preheat the oven to 400°F. In a large bowl, combine the cauliflower florets, salt, and sesame oil. Toss everything together, ensuring each piece of cauliflower is well-coated. This step not only seasons the cauliflower but also helps it roast evenly and develop a beautiful golden color.

Spread the cauliflower out in a cast-iron skillet or on a baking sheet. Don't overcrowd the pan; you want each piece to have enough space to roast properly. Roast for about 15 minutes. You're looking for the cauliflower to be tender when pierced with a fork, with some nice caramelized spots. The cauliflower should still have some bite to it; we're not aiming for mushy here!

While the cauliflower is roasting, prepare the goma dressing. Use a suribachi if possible, or a regular mortar and pestle. Start by grinding the sesame seeds. Be careful not to overgrind; aim for a coarse meal, not a paste. If you notice a few whole seeds hanging out, that's totally fine. Transfer the ground seeds to a bowl. (If you're using a suribachi, use a pastry brush to coax the seeds out of the grooves.) Add the soy sauce and sugar, then mix everything together with a rubber spatula until a thick, fragrant dressing forms. The consistency should be similar to wet sand.

CONTINUED →

CAULIFLOWER GOMA-AE, CONTINUED

As soon as the cauliflower is finished roasting, take it out of the oven and allow it to cool to room temperature. Transfer the roasted cauliflower to the bowl with the dressing and use the rubber spatula to gently fold everything together, making sure each floret is well-coated with dressing. Work gently to avoid breaking up the cauliflower too much. (Transfer the cauliflower to a bowl to coat with the dressing, if that's easier.)

Serve immediately, or refrigerate for up to a week; bring it back to room temperature before serving.

P.S. This dish also works really well with quickly sautéed asparagus. As with the cauliflower, don't overcook, you want the asparagus nice and crunchy.

BRAISED HIJIKI

煮ひじき

Hijiki is a kind of brown seaweed that grows wild on the rocky coastlines of Japan and has been a staple of the country's cuisine for thousands of years. Hijiki, especially when traditionally braised in a flavorful, savory-sweet cooking liquid like we do here, is a perfect complement to other dishes, be it for breakfast, lunch, or dinner. It's also packed with loads of minerals and nutrients. And just so you know, there's been a brouhaha about arsenic in hijiki, but we don't worry about it; soaking and cooking the hijiki like we do here removes it, plus you'd have to eat a dump-truck-full of hijiki to start thinking about this—the servings here are fine. We love *nagahijiki* ("long hijiki"), the stem part of the plant that has a robust, chewy texture. But the stems can be up to 10 inches long, so make sure to cut them into bite-size pieces; your diners will thank you. The other, more common variety is *mehijiki*, which is the tender leaf section of the seaweed, and equally delicious. You'll love hijiki either way, promise.

CONTINUED →

BRAISED HIJIKI, CONTINUED

SERVES 4

½ cup dried hijiki

2 pieces abura age (deep-fried tofu)

1 tablespoon vegetable oil

1 small carrot, thinly sliced into matchsticks (about ¼ cup)

½ cup dashi (page 40)

2 tablespoons soy sauce

1 tablespoon sugar

1 tablespoon mirin

Toasted sesame seeds for garnish

In a medium bowl, combine the dried hijiki with enough cold water to cover. Let it soak for 30 minutes to reconstitute. Drain the hijiki well in a colander, pressing out excess water with your hands. (If using *nagahijiki*, roughly chop the long pieces into about 1-inch lengths for easier eating.)

While the hijiki is soaking, prepare the abura age. Place the abura age pieces in a colander in the sink. Pour boiling water over them to remove excess oil from both sides. Use chopsticks to press out excess water and let sit until cool enough to handle. Slice the abura age into thin strips and set aside.

Create an *otoshibuta,* or drop lid (see page 210), by folding a piece of aluminum foil into a circle slightly smaller than the diameter of your pot. Set aside.

In a medium saucepan or Dutch oven, heat the vegetable oil over medium heat. Add the hijiki and cook, stirring constantly, for about 2 minutes. This initial sautéing helps the hijiki maintain its shape during braising.

Add the carrot and cook, stirring frequently, for 1 minute. Pour in the dashi, soy sauce, sugar, and mirin. Add the abura age. Stir to combine, then place the otoshibuta on top of the ingredients. Reduce the heat to medium-low and let simmer for 15 minutes.

Remove the otoshibuta and give everything a gentle stir to ensure even cooking. Replace the otoshibuta and continue cooking for 5 minutes more. (Using the otoshibuta ensures that everything is cooked through evenly.)

Finally, remove the otoshibuta and continue cooking, uncovered, for about 5 minutes, or until most of the liquid has evaporated and the hijiki is glossy and well-coated with the braising liquid. (You don't want soupy hijiki.) You should smell a rich, savory aroma, and the hijiki should look dark and glistening.

Transfer to a serving bowl and let cool to room temperature before serving. Garnish with a sprinkle of toasted sesame seeds. Braised hijiki can be stored in an airtight container in the refrigerator for up to a week. It's incredibly versatile—enjoy hijiki hot, at room temperature, or cold straight from the fridge.

5

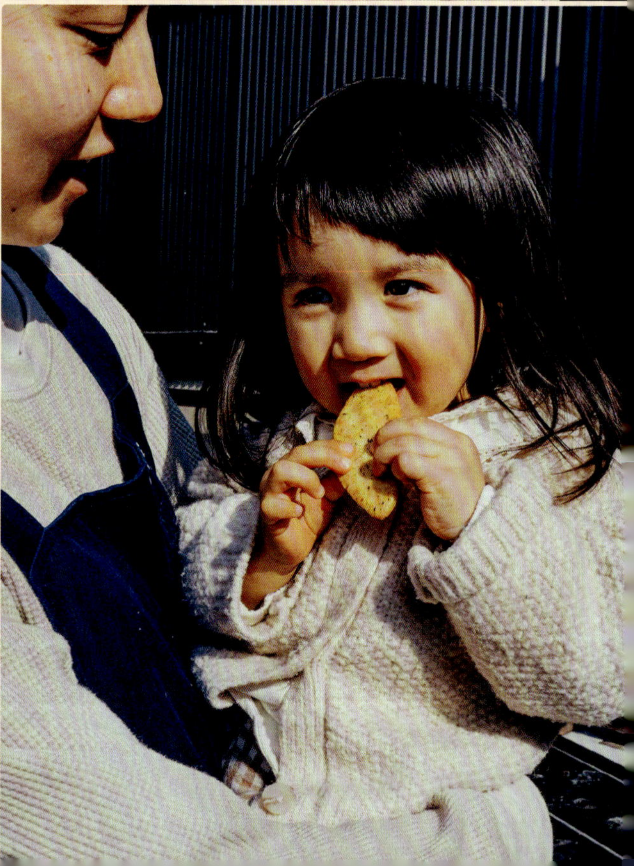

[MORE AMAZING]

VEGETABLES

野菜

Reverence for vegetables is tightly woven into Japanese cuisine and culture. The country's topography is defined by mountains and forests, with precious little land available for farming. Farmers tend miniscule plots that are, even to this day, often handed down through the generations. But while the plots are small, sometimes no bigger than five acres, the output is mighty. Farmers vary the veggies they grow on a single plot, including eggplant, cucumber, and taro, originally introduced a thousand years ago by Chinese Buddhist monks; cabbage, sweet potato, and pumpkin first brought to Japan by Portuguese and Dutch traders four hundred years ago; and more recent arrivals like tomatoes, corn, asparagus, broccoli, and lettuce, which took root over the past century and a half.

Japan's rugged terrain and varied climate led to specialized vegetable varieties suited to local growing conditions, while cities themselves became urban agricultural zones. Kyoto farmers grow their own bespoke eggplant, carrots, and green onions (collectively known as *kyo yasai,* officially designated Kyoto heirloom vegetables), while Tokyo farmers are known for their daikon, ginger, and sweet onion, all adapted to the city's particular climate. (If you break away from the tourist trail, you can still find these urban farms going strong in both cities.)

Vegetables are so integral to Japanese culture that a thousand years ago, young samurai studied vegetable cultivation along with swordsmanship (perhaps pulling deep-rooted veggies like daikon and burdock helped build katana-swinging muscles). And Buddhist monks evolved a unique all-vegetarian cooking style based on their spiritual practice (see page 139).

The twin pillars of Japanese vegetable cooking are seasonality and freshness, a sensibility expressed as *shun,* the peak flavor of a particular vegetable, the point at which a vegetable tastes the best it can possibly be. This foundational idea is so ingrained in the nation's consciousness that everyone from grandmas to schoolkids can rattle off the shun of everything from bamboo shoots to sweet potatoes.

The key to cooking vegetables the Japanese way is this: Less is more. Simple comforting cooking, highlighting beautiful natural flavors, not beating the crap out of them with heavy seasonings and spices—that's the way to go.

We love vegetables, which is why we added two full chapters on them in this book! The recipes that follow range from traditional to modern, but all hew to the singular Japanese approach to this cooking.

(And don't forget our all-vegetarian noodle dishes in the noodle section! Try Kinoko Soba, page 82; Goma Dare Soba, page 84; Kimchi Ramen, vegetarian variation, page 87; and Veggie Curry Ramen, page 89.)

NAPA
CABBAGE
DAIKON
KABOCHA
LOTUS
ROOT
BURDOCK
ROOT (GOBO)
SHUNGIKU
SHIMEJI
MUSHROOMS
TARO ROOT
(SATOIMO)
MAITAKE
MUSHROOMS
SHIITAKE
MUSHROOMS
SHISO
JAPANESE
EGGPLANT

YASAi FUTOMAKi

(GIANT VEGETARIAN SUSHI ROLLS)

野菜太巻き

These fat sushi rolls, up to 2½ inches in diameter and filled with loads of tasty ingredients (sometimes ten or more!), are incredibly popular, sold in konbini (see page 103) and train stations, or prepared at home, where families boast their favorite combos. This version is 100 percent vegetarian (*yasai* means "vegetables"), but futomaki is also prepared with *tamagoyaki* (rolled Japanese omelet), freshwater or saltwater eel, minced fish, and other ingredients. Futomaki are easy to make, but you have to practice the technique a bit. Don't get discouraged if it takes a few tries. Stick with it! Since we're using only vegetables, we're flavoring the shiitake and abura age (fried tofu sheets) with Japanese seasonings to boost the mouthwatering umami. And let's talk practical stuff for a quick sec: If the roll feels loose, use your mat to gently squeeze it back together before continuing. If filling spills out the sides, reduce the amount of filling or go gentler on your mat. And if the cuts aren't clean, sharpen your damn knife!

MAKES 2 ROLLS (ABOUT 16 PIECES)

4 cups prepared sushi rice (see page 150)

SHIITAKE

8 fresh medium shiitake mushrooms (about 1 cup when sliced)

2 tablespoons sake

1 tablespoon soy sauce

1½ teaspoons sugar

ABURA AGE

2 pieces abura age (deep-fried tofu)

Boiling water, for rinsing the abura

2 tablespoons sake

1½ teaspoons mirin

1½ teaspoons soy sauce

VEGETABLES

1 small bunch spinach (about 4 ounces), stems trimmed

1 medium carrot, scrubbed, cut in half lengthwise, and halves into thirds lengthwise

1 (6- to 7-inch) Japanese or Persian cucumber, unpeeled, cut in half lengthwise, and halves into thirds lengthwise

1 ripe but firm avocado, cut into ¼-inch-thick strips

ASSEMBLY

2 sheets nori (about 8 by 7 inches)

Soy sauce and wasabi, for serving

Prepare the sushi rice ahead of time and allow it to come to room temperature. (Important: Don't put the sushi rice in the refrigerator. It will clump up, lose flavor, and be impossible to work with. It can sit for a while at room temperature and it'll be fine.)

Prepare the shiitake. Remove the stems and slice the caps into thin strips. Place all the ingredients in a medium skillet over medium heat. Cook, stirring occasionally, until the liquid evaporates and the mushrooms are tender and glossy, 4 to 5 minutes.

Prepare the abura age. Place the abura age pieces in a colander in the sink. Pour boiling water over them to remove excess oil from both sides. Use chopsticks to press out excess water, then let sit until cool to the touch. Slice the abura age into thin strips and set aside.

In a small skillet, combine the sake, mirin, soy sauce, and 2 tablespoons of water. Add the sliced abura age, bring to a simmer over medium heat, and cook until most of the liquid is absorbed, about 1 minute. Cool completely before using.

CONTINUED →

YASAI FUTOMAKI, CONTINUED

Bring a pot of water to a boil over medium-high heat and prepare an ice bath. Blanch the spinach for about 30 seconds until it just turns bright green. Transfer to the ice bath until it cools. Squeeze dry and set aside. Using the same boiling water, cook the carrots for about 2 minutes until soft. Transfer to the ice bath, drain, and pat dry.

Set up a rolling station: Cover a bamboo mat with plastic wrap. Prepare a small bowl of warm water for moistening your hands and have all the fillings within easy reach. Keep a damp kitchen towel nearby for wiping your knife between cuts.

For each roll, first create the filling layer: Place the nori shiny-side down on the bamboo mat. The mat should be positioned so you're rolling from a short side of the rectangle. Moisten your hands with water and spread about 2 cups of sushi rice evenly over the nori, leaving 2 inches of nori exposed on the side farthest away from you. The rice layer should be about ¼ inch thick. Arrange the spinach, carrots, cucumber, avocado, shiitake, and abura age on top of the rice, one next to the other. Be careful not to overfill; less is more when it comes to futomaki fillings.

Roll the futomaki. Using the mat, lift the bottom edge up and over the fillings. Keep your fingers on top of the mat to hold the ingredients in place. The first fold should completely enclose the fillings; think of wrapping a package. Pull back slightly on the mat while continuing to roll forward, maintaining even pressure along the entire length. Moisten the exposed nori edge to seal the roll. Complete the roll by pressing gently but firmly along its length using the mat.

Using a very sharp knife moistened with warm water, trim the ends of the roll. Cut the roll in half, then each half into quarters, wiping the blade clean between every cut. Repeat for the other roll.

Arrange the pieces cut-side up on a serving plate to showcase the cross-section of vegetables. Serve immediately with soy sauce and wasabi for dipping.

P.S. You can prepare all the components and vegetables (except the avocado) up to a day in advance. Refrigerate separately. Bring the rice to room temperature before rolling, and cut the avocado just before assembly.

KABOCHA NIMONO
(SIMMERED KABOCHA PUMPKIN)
南瓜煮物

In this traditional recipe, kabocha pumpkin is simmered in a flavorful cooking liquid to enhance the gourd's natural sweetness, a classic cooking technique (one of the big five, see page 15). While kabocha is known as a Japanese variety, it was actually introduced to the country by Portuguese traders in the 1600s and is thought to have been an import from Cambodia, where Portuguese ships also landed. In fact, the name *kabocha* is believed to come from "Camboja," the Portuguese word for the origin country. Another fun fact: Kabocha needs to ripen for a month or two after harvest to allow time for its starches to convert to sugar. So if you're able to nab a kabocha at your local farmers' market, let it sit in a cool, dark spot for a few weeks before cooking. Now, not so much a fun fact, but an important one: Kabocha is difficult to cut because its skin is so tough. So carefully make an incision with the heaviest knife you own and then continue to cut it from the soft flesh side instead of the tough skin side. Finally, you'll see quite a bit of sugar added to the cooking liquid. The purpose here is to tease out the sweet flavor of the pumpkin (see page 126 for why); only a tiny bit of the cooking liquid is consumed.

SERVES 4

2 pounds kabocha pumpkin (if you can't find kabocha, use butternut, acorn, or another winter squash)

4 cups water

⅓ cup sugar

½ teaspoon salt

2 tablespoons soy sauce

Form an otoshibuta (drop lid) from aluminum foil and set aside (see page 210).

Carefully cut the kabocha into approximately 1½-inch cubes. Here's how: The pumpkin is hard, so use a sharp knife and a stable cutting board. Cut the kabocha in half, tip to tail, starting from the bottom (it's easier this way). Also cut out the stem if there is one. Scoop out the seeds. Partially peel the skin to allow the cooking liquid to be absorbed, but leave on some skin for color and texture. (You can and should eat the skin.) Now cut the kabocha into cubes from the *flesh side* of the squash.

Arrange the kabocha pieces in a single layer in a heavy-bottomed pot (an enameled cast-iron pot or Dutch oven is ideal; this helps the kabocha maintain its shape during cooking. Add the water and bring to a boil over high heat.

CONTINUED →

KABOCHA NIMONO, CONTINUED

Reduce the heat to a simmer and skim off any foam that appears on the surface. Add the sugar and place the otoshibuta on top of the kabocha (you don't have to mix; the otoshibuta takes care of circulating the liquid). Simmer for 5 minutes. The kabocha will begin to soften and take on a vibrant orange color.

Add the salt and soy sauce. Continue to simmer for 10 more minutes. At this point, the kabocha should be tender. Test it with a chopstick or fork; it should pierce easily but still hold its shape. Turn off the heat and let the kabocha sit in the cooking liquid for about 30 minutes. During this time, it will absorb more flavor and cool to room temperature.

Serve the kabocha either in a big serving bowl or in individual bowls. Spoon a little bit of the cooking liquid over the kabocha.

P.S. Leftover kabocha can be stored in the cooking liquid in the refrigerator for up to a week, which will allow the flavors to develop further. (Nimono dishes always taste better the next day!) Eat it cold, or gently reheated.

"SA SHI SU SE SO"

The order in which we add seasonings to cook kabocha nimono and other dishes isn't willy-nilly. There's an intent to it, which is revealed by the mnemonic "Sa Shi Su Se So." These represent the five essential flavor elements in Japanese cuisine:

- "Sa," or sugar (*sato*), is added first to allow time to penetrate ingredients.
- "Shi," or salt (*shio*), is added next to enhance flavors.
- "Su," or vinegar (*su*), adds acidity and helps balance flavors.
- "Se," or soy sauce (*shoyu*), bestows umami and saltiness and is added later in cooking to prevent over-reduction.
- "So," or miso, contributes complex umami flavors but is heat-sensitive, so it's added at the end to preserve flavor and aroma.

The fundamental idea here is that you add these seasonings in this specific order when you're cooking (i.e., sugar, then salt, etc.). Why? Because—centuries before food science was a thing—Japanese cooks learned empirically that this sequence of additions creates the balanced flavor profile that is central to Japanese cuisine. Practically, for example, if you add salt before sugar, the sugar wouldn't be able to be absorbed by the ingredients. And if you add miso, the strongest flavor, too early, it will drown out all the other notes in the dish. Whew, this is a bit theoretical but important to understand. You'll see that we follow this order in all our recipes, even if we don't call it out. Finally, even though they're not part of the core concept, sake and mirin are also crucial seasonings that add depth and umami to dishes.

NASU DENGAKU

茄子田楽

This is another fantastic dish associated with Buddhist vegetarian cooking, like Agedashi Tofu (page 133), thought to have been invented by monks back in the 1600s. Traditionally, eggplant was roasted over *binchotan* (pure oak) charcoal and topped with a sweet-savory miso glaze. We cook the contemporary version on the stovetop with American eggplant (officially called globe eggplant), but you can use any variety you dig up. If you can find them, we love Japanese eggplants for this dish, naturally; they are thinner and longer than the fat American kind and have a beautiful creamy texture. (Just be sure to slice them in half lengthwise.)

SERVES 4

¼ cup hatcho miso

2 tablespoons sugar

3 tablespoons sake

2 tablespoons mirin

1 large globe eggplant (about 1 pound)

2 tablespoons sesame oil

1 teaspoon toasted white sesame seeds

In a small saucepan, combine the hatcho miso (if the miso is hard, combine it with a little water before adding it to the saucepan), sugar, sake, and mirin. Cook over low heat, whisking continuously, until the miso dissolves, 2 to 3 minutes, and it's thick and glossy. The consistency should be akin to a thick tomato puree. Set aside.

Cut the eggplant into 1-inch-thick rounds. If the eggplant is huge, cut the rounds in half or even into quarters to make them easier to handle with a fork or chopsticks. In a large bowl, combine the eggplant with enough water to cover and let soak for about 5 minutes to remove bitterness. Drain the eggplant and pat dry with paper towels.

In a large cast-iron skillet, heat the sesame oil over medium-high heat. When the oil is hot, lay in the eggplant pieces. Cook, undisturbed, until they start to brown, about 5 minutes. Reduce the heat to low and flip the eggplant. Continue cooking for another 5 minutes or until the eggplant is completely cooked through and tender inside (test by piercing with a chopstick).

Spoon the miso sauce over each piece. Don't use a brush; a spoon allows you to add more sauce and creates a better coating. Sprinkle generously with the sesame seeds and serve immediately, directly from the pan.

ROASTED VEGETABLES IN PONZU

焼き野菜とポン酢

Roasting vegetables is an adaptation of a classic Western cooking technique, except in this case you're tossing veggies in fragrant toasted sesame oil instead of olive oil. Simple enough, caramelized and delicious (roasting concentrates the vegetable's flavor), and perfect for a quick side to complement whatever else you're whipping up. While certainly nice on their own, when these veggies are paired with ponzu, then you've got magic happening. A vinegary, citrusy condiment bursting with umami, bright acid, and lip-smacking flavor, ponzu is a versatile flavoring that can also add pop to grilled fish, chicken, or beef. Or you can use it instead of the dressings in the cucumber and wakame recipe (see page 111), or toss it with tomatoes and greens and a little olive oil for a rapid insta-salad (see page 109). Word of advice here: While bottled ponzu is available online or at Asian markets—don't buy it. Most (though not all) commercial ponzu is ultra-processed and loaded with garbage. Make your own! It's so easy. Mix a few ingredients together, let them meld for a day, and presto—ponzu. (And ponzu will last for a couple of weeks in the fridge.) Our recipe is for an all-vegetarian variety, but we offer another classic variation as well (see page 130). And besides the components we list, this recipe works well with basically any vegetable that can be roasted: green beans, wax beans, butternut squash, kabocha, Brussels sprouts, bell peppers, okra. Mix and match as you like; think roughly a pound and a half of veggies for four people. Just make sure harder vegetables are cut slightly smaller than tender ones so everything cooks evenly. (The rangiri cutting technique, see page 209, comes in super handy here.) Finally, we call for grated daikon (daikon oroshi) mixed with ponzu and fiery yuzu kosho to add another bold flavor kick. The grated daikon also helps the ponzu sauce adhere to the veggies. But if you don't have time or can't find daikon, go to town with just the veggies and ponzu!

SERVES 4

PONZU

2 tablespoons mirin

¼ cup citrus juice (yuzu, lemon, lime, or a combination)

2 tablespoons rice vinegar

½ cup soy sauce

2 tablespoons water

1 (2-inch) square kombu

2 dried shiitake mushrooms

Prepare the ponzu a day ahead. In a small saucepan, bring the mirin to a boil over medium-high heat to cook off the alcohol. As soon as it boils, turn off the heat and let it cool. In a medium bowl, combine the cooled mirin, the citrus juice, rice vinegar, soy sauce, water, kombu, and shiitake. Cover and refrigerate overnight to let the flavors meld. Remove the kombu and shiitake (squeeze out the liquid from the shiitake) and transfer the ponzu to a jar with a lid. It will keep refrigerated for up to 2 weeks.

CONTINUED →

ROASTED VEGETABLES IN PONZU, CONTINUED

VEGETABLES

1 cup broccoli florets, cut into small pieces

1 cup cauliflower florets, cut into small pieces

1 cup chopped zucchini, cut into ½-inch-thick rounds

1 cup chopped Japanese eggplant, cut into ½-inch-thick rounds

½ cup chopped carrots, cut into ¼-inch-thick rounds

2 tablespoons sesame oil

½ teaspoon salt

¼ cup grated daikon, skin and all, excess daikon liquid squeezed out (drink it, it's good for you!)

1 teaspoon red yuzu kosho

Preheat the oven to 400°F.

In a large bowl, toss the broccoli, cauliflower, zucchini, eggplant, and carrots with the sesame oil and salt. Spread the vegetables in a single layer on a large baking sheet. Arrange the different vegetables separately for both practical reasons (see the next step) and aesthetic appeal (serve them that way)—just make sure they're not overcrowded for proper roasting.

Roast until the vegetables are cooked through but still have some bite to them, about 20 minutes. There should be some caramelization on the outside and they should maintain their shape and not be mushy. Use your judgment. Since they're separated on the pan, if, say, the zucchini is ready but the carrots need more time, scoop out the zucchini but leave the carrots in for a couple more minutes.

While the vegetables are roasting, combine the grated daikon with the yuzu kosho and ponzu and divide among four small bowls.

When the vegetables are ready, serve them family-style on a large platter, with each vegetable separated. Serve with the ponzu mixture on the side. Dip the roasted veggies in the bowl to eat. Yummy!

PONZU VARIATION WITH KATSUOBUSHI

Here's another classic ponzu, called *dashi-pon* in Japan, this one boosted with umami-rich, smoky *katsuobushi* (dried, shaved bonito—the key ingredient of classic dashi). Simply substitute ¼ cup katsuobushi for the shiitake mushrooms. Let it sit overnight to meld, then strain the liquid before transferring it to an airtight container. It's not 100 percent vegetarian, but it's 100 percent delicious, with a bold flavor. If you're so inclined, give it a try!

AGEDASHI TOFU

揚げだし豆腐

Although this isn't technically a main course, it shouldn't be missed. A dish first mentioned in a cookbook from the 1700s, agedashi has become firmly ensconced in the Japanese culinary playbook, a popular side dish served everywhere from *izakayas* (eating pubs) to hallowed *kaiseki* restaurants to the dinner table at home. It's easy to see why. The tofu here is deep-fried to create a light, crispy exterior that gives way to a silky center, then bathed in a savory-sweet dashi broth, with a trio of fresh garnishes at the end to give a pop of flavor. Texture, flavor, aroma—so much going on. It complements fish, chicken, vegetables, you name it. You'll notice, too, that one of the toppings is grated daikon, which you often see with deep-fried Japanese dishes. That's not by accident. Besides adding beautiful fresh, slightly peppery flavor and helping the dashi broth adhere to the tofu, the enzymes in daikon help you digest oily foods, making for a more pleasant dining (and post-dining) experience. The recipe calls for squeezing the liquid from the grated daikon—but make sure to drink it! It's packed with nutrients, refreshing and delicious. A little reward for the cook.

SERVES 4

1 (14-ounce) package firm tofu

1 cup dashi, traditional or shiitake (see pages 40 and 43)

¼ cup usukuchi soy sauce

2 tablespoons mirin

Vegetable oil for deep-frying

½ cup potato starch (katakuriko)

2 tablespoons grated daikon, skin and all, excess water squeezed out

1 tablespoon freshly grated ginger

2 tablespoons Shibori Scallions (page 41)

Drain the tofu, put it on a plate lined with paper towels, and place in the sink. Set another plate on top of the tofu and weigh it down with a can or a small skillet. Press the tofu this way for about 15 minutes to remove excess moisture and prepare the tofu for deep-frying. When the tofu is ready, pat it dry and cut it into 12 pieces. Set aside.

While the tofu drains, in a small saucepan, create a dashi broth by combining the dashi, soy sauce, and mirin. Bring to a boil over medium heat, then turn off the heat.

Fill a large, heavy-bottomed skillet with oil to a depth of 2 inches and heat over medium-high heat. Choose a vessel with a lot of surface area so the tofu has room to cook and the oil temperature remains stable. (We used an 11-inch stainless steel skillet, which worked great; cast iron is also fantastic.)

CONTINUED →

AGEDASHI TOFU, CONTINUED

Meanwhile, lightly dredge each tofu cube in potato starch, shaking off any excess. The coating should be very thin and even. Line a plate with paper towels and set it close to the stove.

Test the oil temperature by tossing in a tiny pinch of potato starch. If the starch bubbles furiously, the oil is ready. Use a spider or slotted spoon to carefully lower the coated tofu into the hot oil, working in batches if necessary to avoid overcrowding the skillet, which will lower the oil temperature. Fry for about 6 minutes, turning once and using tongs or kitchen chopsticks to keep the tofu pieces separated, until the exterior is pale tan (*kitsune,* or the color of a fox) and crispy. Keep an eye on the tofu as it cooks; if it's browning too quickly, lower the heat a bit. Transfer the fried tofu to the paper towels to drain.

About halfway through frying the tofu, reheat the dashi over low heat to warm it up.

To serve, gently place three tofu cubes in each of four small bowls. Ladle about ¼ cup of the warm dashi sauce over and around the tofu. Top each serving with small mounds of grated daikon and grated ginger. Sprinkle the scallions over the tofu and serve immediately. To eat, mix the daikon and ginger into the dashi broth.

VARIATIONS

Agedashi also works great with Japanese eggplant or taro root. Substitute either of these for the tofu and follow the recipe above. Cut the eggplant (which is roughly shaped like a banana) into 2-inch pieces; peel and slice the taro root in half lengthwise.

YASAI ITAME

(STIR-FRIED VEGETABLES)

野菜炒め

Perfect for your weeknight dinner playbook, yasai itame tastes amazing and comes together in minutes. *Itame* means "stir-frying." Here it's veggies (*yasai*) leveled up with traditional Japanese seasonings and aromatics. We use spinach here, but this method works with any leafy green, like bok choy, yu choy, collard greens, mustard greens, Swiss chard, kale, or sweet potato greens (so good, find them in Asian markets). Broccoli also works but cut it up into small florets and add an extra minute or two of cooking time. You also might need extra time with the heartier greens like the collards or Swiss chard. Use your judgment and taste the greens to check for doneness (always taste your cooking). And add a splash of water if the pan is starting to look dry before the veggies are finished. Pro tip: Have all your ingredients measured and ready by the stove (mise en place, as chefs say); this dish cooks so quickly you won't have time to chop and measure once you start.

SERVES 4

1 bunch spinach (about 1 pound), with stems if possible

1½ teaspoons sesame oil

1 teaspoon finely chopped ginger

1 teaspoon finely chopped garlic

¼ teaspoon tobanjan (make it ½ teaspoon if you like heat)

1 tablespoon sake

2 teaspoons soy sauce

Trim any tough ends from the spinach and cut into bite-size pieces. (Make sure to keep the tender stems—they add texture and nutrition.) Wash thoroughly in several changes of water to remove any grit.

Heat a large skillet or wok over medium heat. When the pan is hot, add the sesame oil, ginger, garlic, and tobanjan. Cook for about 30 seconds, stirring constantly to prevent the garlic from burning and to let the tobanjan toast slightly and release its fragrance.

Increase the heat to medium-high and add the spinach (it will seem like a lot but will cook down significantly). Using tongs or cooking chopsticks, lift and turn the greens to help them wilt evenly and come in contact with the aromatics at the bottom of the pan. Once the spinach begins to wilt, about 30 seconds, add the sake and soy sauce.

Continue cooking and stirring for about 1 minute, until most of the liquid has evaporated and the spinach is bright green and tender but still has some bite. The goal is to have the greens just cooked through with almost no liquid remaining in the pan.

Transfer to a serving plate immediately to prevent overcooking. The spinach should be glossy and well-coated with the sauce but not swimming in liquid.

GOBO KARAAGE

(BURDOCK "FRIES")

牛蒡唐揚げ

We came across burdock karaage—marinated and potato-starch-dredged deep-fried burdock root—at a down-home spot called Yaguya in the hip, artsy Kichijoji neighborhood of Tokyo. The chef there, Yoshie Yaguchi, is doing her amazing thing, cooking traditional comfort food with a decidedly modern vibe. (Her husband, Yosuke, manages the front-of-house, by the way; they might be the most adorable restaurant couple in Tokyo.) *Karaage* (pronounced "karra-agh-eh") usually means "deep-fried chicken," but Chef Yoshie applies the same technique to burdock root, with spectacular results. So, of course, we had to share this recipe inspired by her fun dish, which makes a great snack or rounds out a meal. For extra oomph, the crunchy sticks of burdock root are dusted in sea salt, white pepper, and robust *aonori* (pronounced "ah-oh-nori"), the flaky version of the nori seaweed that wraps your favorite sushi rolls. Forget french fries; this checks all the boxes, seriously.

SERVES 4

½ pound burdock root (about ¾ of a root; save the rest for miso soup)

2 tablespoons soy sauce

1 teaspoon sugar

½ teaspoon freshly grated garlic

3 tablespoons potato starch (katakuriko)

Vegetable oil for deep frying

½ teaspoon sea salt

¼ teaspoon ground white pepper

2 teaspoons aonori (powdered seaweed)

Prepare a bowl filled with cold water. Under cold running water, use steel wool or a scrubby to gently rub off the brown outer layer of the burdock root (it doesn't have to be perfect). Cut the burdock into 2-inch-long, ½-inch-wide sticks and immediately place them in the water to prevent discoloration.

In a bowl, combine soy sauce, sugar, and grated garlic. Drain the burdock sticks and pat dry with paper towels. Add them to the soy sauce mixture and stir well to coat. Marinate for about 5 minutes.

Add the potato starch to the marinated burdock. Mix thoroughly to coat each piece evenly. The starch should adhere to the burdock, creating a light coating.

CONTINUED →

GOBO KARAAGE, CONTINUED

Prepare a deep-fry station. (Important: Read our note on deep-frying first, see page 213.) Fill a large cast-iron skillet (ideal) with at least 1½ inches of oil, enough so that the burdock will float when it cooks. Attach a deep-fry or candy thermometer to the side of the skillet and heat the oil to 330°F over medium heat. It's crucial to use a thermometer to maintain the correct temperature throughout the frying process. On a work surface near the burner, prepare a paper towel–lined plate to drain the cooked burdock.

When the oil is ready, shake off any excess marinade—it will cause the oil to splatter—and use a spider or slotted spoon to carefully lower the burdock into the hot oil, working in batches if necessary to avoid overcrowding the skillet, which will lower the oil temperature. Fry for about 5 minutes, until the burdock turns golden brown and crispy, like the color of french fries. Adjust the heat throughout the frying time to maintain the temperature at 330°F. Transfer the fried burdock with a slotted spoon to the prepared plate.

Toss with the salt, white pepper, and aonori so the burdock is well-seasoned and serve piping hot.

SHOJIN RYORI, BUDDHIST VEGETARIAN CUISINE

Shojin ryori, literally "devotion cuisine," is the cooking that emerged from Buddhist temples over a thousand years ago. It avoids all animals—no meat, no fish—to adhere to the Buddhist precepts against killing living beings, and also avoids pungent ingredients like garlic and onions, which were thought to interfere with meditation. Shun, which we discuss earlier, is super important in this cooking. And shojin follows the "rule of five," emphasizing five colors, five flavors, and five cooking methods in meals. By mixing and matching these sets of five, you're by definition eating healthy, delicious, and beautiful food. Tofu, mushrooms, roots, leafy greens, seaweed, and *sansai* (wild mountain vegetables) are all central to this cooking, along with rice, of course, and key flavorings like miso and sesame oil. Modern comfort cooking embraces shojin classics, including Nasu Dengaku (page 128) and Agedashi Tofu (page 133), which we feature in this chapter. (And don't forget Kenchin Jiru in the soup chapter, page 49.)

VEGETABLE KUSHI-AGE

野菜串揚げ

Deep-fried food on a stick? What's not to love? Kushi-age are panko-breaded-and-fried skewers. *Kushi* refers to a particular kind of bamboo skewer, while *age* ("ag-eh," with a hard "g") means "fried," one of the five fundamental Japanese cooking techniques, or goho. While this dish is now super popular all across Japan, it's to Osaka what Fenway Franks are to, well, Fenway Park (shout-out to our Boston peeps!). In Osaka, a mind-blowing food city, by the way, you'll find kushi-age (locals like to call it *kushikatsu*) everywhere, whether at a hole-in-the-wall at the central train station or at a specialized haute-cuisine operation where a chef in crisp whites hands you one precious skewer at a time. Kushi-age was created in the 1920s as an affordable, convenient meal for blue-collar workers in Osaka's Shinsekai district to chow down on with a bunch of friends and a beer or three. And that's the vibe we're going after here with this recipe. While kushi-age is prepared with various ingredients, like meat, seafood, and vegetables, we're sticking to vegetables here. Why? Simple: We love vegetables! Sweet potatoes, lotus root, burdock root, Brussels sprouts, cauliflower, bell peppers, mushrooms, and green beans work great with this recipe. (Use this method for shrimp, white-fleshed fish, or pork, too, if the mood strikes you.) Kushi-age is typically served with a tangy Worcester-based dipping sauce and cabbage on the side, which helps you digest oily foods (see page 133 for more on this). This is the perfect party food—fun to prepare and eat with friends and family.

SERVES 4

VEGETABLES

1 red onion, quartered

1 head broccoli, cut into 1-inch florets

1 zucchini, cut into ½-inch-thick rounds

1 Japanese eggplant, cut into ½-inch-thick rounds

20 (5-inch) bamboo skewers (for everything except asparagus)

8 asparagus spears, trimmed and the hard end peeled if thick

Prepare the vegetables. For the onion, separate the quartered pieces into individual layers that will hold their shape when skewered. The broccoli florets should be uniform in size, to ensure even cooking. Skewer the vegetables, except the asparagus, by threading two pieces of each onto a bamboo skewer, leaving enough space at the bottom to hold the skewer. Set aside on a plate.

Make the dipping sauce. In a small bowl, combine the Worcestershire sauce, water, soy sauce, and tobanjan. Mix well until the tobanjan is fully incorporated. Set aside.

Make the batter. In a medium bowl, whisk together the egg, flour, water, and rice vinegar until smooth and thin like pancake batter. Pour the panko breadcrumbs on a plate. And prepare a clean plate for the breaded vegetables.

CONTINUED →

DIPPING SAUCE

¼ cup Worcestershire sauce

2 tablespoons water

1 tablespoon soy sauce

½ teaspoon tobanjan

BATTER

1 egg

½ cup all-purpose flour

¼ cup water

2 teaspoons rice vinegar

BREADING

2 cups panko breadcrumbs

Vegetable oil for deep-frying

Shichimi togarashi, for serving (optional)

Prepare a deep-fry station. (Important: Read our note on deep-frying first, see page 213.) Fill a large cast-iron skillet or heavy-bottomed pot with 2 inches of oil, enough so that the vegetables will float when they cook. Attach a deep-fry or candy thermometer to the side of the skillet and heat the oil to 330°F over medium heat. It's crucial to use a thermometer to maintain the correct temperature throughout the frying process. On a work surface near the burner, prepare a paper towel–lined plate to drain the cooked vegetables.

Meanwhile, bread the vegetables. Dip each skewer into the batter, making sure it's evenly coated, and then roll it in the panko breadcrumbs. Use your hands to press the breadcrumbs firmly onto the vegetables to ensure they stick. For the asparagus, follow the same breading process but without skewering. Place the breaded vegetables on the clean plate.

When the oil is ready, carefully add several skewers, being careful not to overcrowd, and fry for about 2 minutes on each side, until golden brown and crispy. The vegetables should be cooked through but still retain some crunch. Maintain the oil temperature at 330° to 340°F, adjusting the heat as needed.

Transfer the skewers to the prepared plate to drain. For best results, first stand the skewers upright to allow excess oil to drip off. Continue frying in batches until all the vegetables are cooked.

Serve immediately while hot and crispy, with the dipping sauce on the side. Offer shichimi togarashi at the table for those who want an extra kick of spice.

6

FISH

魚

Let's set the table: Japan, a country perched on four main islands and 6,848 smaller ones, claims the world's sixth-longest coastline—one and half times longer than that of the United States. It's a mosaic of inlets, bays, peninsulas, deltas, estuaries, coves, lagoons, and countless ecological niches, from deep trenches to shallow coastal waters—all of which is a dream come true if you happen to be a sea creature. Its particular location in the ocean is fortuitous, too. Japan is situated at the confluence of the Kuroshio and Oyashio, two major ocean currents that serve as basically marine life superhighways, a meeting point that yields one of the world's richest marine ecosystems, supporting some 3,300 species of fish.

The upshot of all this is while shrimp, salmon, and canned tuna are the three most popular seafoods here in the United States, any *average* supermarket in Japan as a matter of course offers a bounty of fresh fish that can include, yes, Pacific salmon that spawns in northern Japan, tuna, skipjack tuna, yellowtail (wild and farmed), monkfish, mackerel, Spanish mackerel, horse mackerel, sardines, sea bream, sea bass, cod, flounder—the list goes on. And on.

Naturally, this bounty of sea life has played a central role in Japanese cooking from prehistory to today, especially since mountains and forests define the geography and arable land is limited. So the Japanese have always looked to the ocean for nourishment (and to lakes and rivers, to a lesser extent), with fish serving as the country's primary protein. The Japanese culinary philosophy of natural flavors, seasonality, and not futzing too much with the food reaches its apex in preparing fish.

The first major fish market in Japan appeared in 1603 in Edo, today's Tokyo, one of the largest cities in the world at the time. Edo cooking evolved bolder, more seasoned fish preparations for both taste and practical reasons; soy sauce, miso, and other fermented ingredients helped prevent spoilage, a critical consideration for a massive metropolis. The area around Kyoto and Osaka, meanwhile, developed more delicate fish dishes.

You'll experience both these traditions in the recipes that follow, preparations that range from raw to broiled to braised, from classic to modern. And because we're talking fish, we're talking quick and easy, and so damn good—we sleep soundly at night knowing you're adding *teriyaki,* broiling three ways, miso-ni, karaage, and more to your cooking playbook. (At least we hope you do!)

IN PRAISE OF OILY FISH

Consider the recipes in this chapter your chance to break out of the salmon–sea bass–halibut hegemony. Expand your piscine horizons—eat more oily fish! Why? Mackerel, Spanish mackerel, sardines, sablefish, bluefish, kingfish, and even freshwater trout are species that contain high levels of fat, hence the "oily" moniker. But that fat ain't bad; it's what makes these fish rich, robust, and delicious, and helps them stay moist and tender when you cook 'em. And beyond how tasty they are, the fat in oily fish is composed of natural omega-3 fatty acids, essential for a healthy heart, eyes, and brain. Good and good for you—woohoo! Japanese cuisine embraces oily fish, and we urge you to give them a try. (And, hey, we bet you already love salmon, right? Well, guess what: Salmon is a card-carrying member of the oily fish club!)

JAPANESE SAKE

This beverage is known in Japan as *nihonshu,* literally "Japanese liquor"—that's how central it's been to the culture for thousands of years. In Shinto rituals, sake is offered to form a spiritual bond with the gods. Kagami-biraki, breaking open sake casks, heralds important celebrations and new beginnings. And in Japanese wedding ceremonies, couples exchange three sips of sake to symbolize their newly formed union.

Sake expresses a mind-blowing spectrum of flavors that span fruity to savory to floral. It balances sweetness, acidity, umami, and astringency, with a mouthfeel that ranges from crisp and sharp to velvety and rounded. Incredibly, all of this is accomplished with just two ingredients: water and rice.

Unlike with wine, where the sugar in grapes is fermented into alcohol, sake faces a more daunting challenge: transforming the starch in rice into alcohol. This is accomplished by a process called parallel simultaneous fermentation. Rice grains are ground down (called "polishing") to remove proteins and oils, leaving just the starchy interior. Once the rice is steamed, it's inoculated with koji mold (see page 22) and yeast. The koji and yeast simultaneously convert the starch and sugar to alcohol and carbon dioxide to create a bubbling mash. This mash is ultimately pressed to squeeze out a clear liquid, sake.

(In ancient times, this same process was achieved by villagers chewing rice and spitting it into a communal tub so the enzymes in the saliva along with natural airborne yeasts could break down the rice's starch!)

This is an oversimplification of an incredibly involved, subtle process that's as much art as science. But you get the general idea. In the hands of a talented *toji* (master sake brewer), this particular alchemy conjures water and rice into thousands of distinct sakes, ones that reflect different types of rice, sources of water, degrees of polishing, production methods, aging, regional preferences, terroir, the personality and philosophy of said toji, and more. This world is deep, deep!

So where to begin? The official premium sake classification system is a good start. Here are the key designations:

- **Junmai** embodies the essence of traditional sake brewing and is characterized by a full-bodied texture and pronounced rice flavors.
- **Ginjo** is known for its fruity, floral, crisp character, with a small amount of added alcohol to accentuate its aromatics.
- **Daiginjo,** the pinnacle of sake craftsmanship, presents a light, complex, elegant flavor profile, with a small amount of added alcohol to boost its aromatic intensity.

Junmai and ginjo are fantastic go-to sakes for everyday sipping, while daiginjo we like to reserve for special occasions.

And here are a few distinct sake styles to sample. These styles encompass the designations above:

- **Yamahai/kimoto:** natural yeast produces a gamey, funky sake with pronounced acidity and depth (one of Tadashi's favorites)
- **Nama:** unpasteurized, just-pressed sake with fresh, lively, and fruity flavors and a vibrant character
- **Genshu:** undiluted sake with a higher alcohol content; powerful and flavorful
- **Nigori:** a cloudy sake with a creamy texture and pronounced rice flavor

The best way to learn about sake is to . . . try different sake styles and producers, and zero in on what you love. Temperature dramatically transforms sake's flavor, too. Try sake lightly chilled; at room temperature; hitohada-kan, literally "body temperature warm," around 95 degrees; or nuru-kan, slightly warmer, around 104 degrees. But don't drink it boiling hot—scorching sake was originally introduced to mask cheap plonk; you lose all the beautiful nuances when it's too hot.

Finally, a note about pairing sake with your meal. Don't. A Japanese meal is a play of dishes that vary in flavors, cooking styles, and more. Think of sake as another component of that meal, to be savored and enjoyed as its own thing, rather than pairing a specific sake with a specific food, as with wine.

TUNA SASHIMI WITH AVOCADO AND KARASHI

鮪さしみとアボカド

Amazing to think that just one hundred years ago tuna was considered *genzakana*, roughly "trash fish." The now-prized *toro* (belly) was considered so unpalatable that the only people who consumed it were poor roustabouts. Ruddy, powerfully flavored tuna flesh was often buried in the ground for four days to ferment in an attempt to improve its taste. (Tuna was once nicknamed *shibi*, which means "four days.") Then refrigeration came along, allowing for wider distribution, tastes evolved, and today, of course, tuna reigns supreme at the sushi counter. This recipe harks back to old days when tuna, shibi or otherwise, was typically paired with sharp karashi mustard (wasabi, a root that grows by mountain streams, was a rare sight back then) to cut the meatiness of the fish (steak au poivre is basically the same idea). And it embraces the now with the addition of avocado, whose richness is the yin to tuna's yang, and Dijon mustard, which adds another flavor layer. The upshot: a modern, incredibly delicious Japanese dish that also drills down to some deep culinary bedrock!

SERVES 4

- ½ pound sashimi-grade tuna
- 1 teaspoon soy sauce
- 1 teaspoon sesame oil
- 2 tablespoons sake
- 1 tablespoon mirin
- 1 tablespoon Dijon mustard
- ½ teaspoon karashi mustard
- ¼ teaspoon salt
- 1 ripe avocado, cut into ½-inch cubes
- 1 tablespoon finely chopped chives (or scallions)

Cut the tuna into ½-inch cubes. In a medium bowl, combine the tuna with the soy sauce and sesame oil. Stir gently and set aside for 5 minutes to marinate.

In a small saucepan, bring the sake and mirin to a boil over medium heat to evaporate the alcohol (a process called *iri sake*). As soon as it boils, remove from the heat and let the liquid cool to room temperature. Once the liquid cools, transfer it to a bowl, add the Dijon mustard, karashi mustard, and salt, and whisk everything together. The sauce should have a smooth, creamy consistency.

Gently stir the avocado into the marinated tuna, being careful not to mash the avocado pieces. Pour in the mustard sauce and fold gently to coat without breaking up the avocado. The sauce should lightly coat each piece of tuna and avocado.

Divide the mixture among four plates, arranging it neatly in the center of each. Garnish with the chopped chives, and serve immediately.

YAKi SABAZUSHi

(GRILLED MACKEREL SUSHI)

焼き鯖鮨

Okay, strap in, we're going deep Japanese culture here. During the Edo Period (1603–1867) the Imperial Court was centered in Kyoto, an inland city surrounded by mountains. But a mainstay of the Japanese diet was fish. So how do you feed the emperor and his hungry retinue in the centuries before refrigerated eighteen-wheelers? Simple: you port the fish, specifically the plentiful mackerel harvested from the Wakasa Bay located forty-five miles northwest of Kyoto, via the "number two bus" (a.k.a. on foot). Hauling fishy loads that could weigh ninety pounds, or more, on their backs, porters followed a series of arduous trails over steep mountain passes and deep valleys that collectively became known as the Saba Kaido, or Mackerel Road. To keep the rich, oily mackerel from fouling during the two to three day journey, the fish was immediately filleted and salted on the beach, and vinegared when it arrived in Kyoto. Naturally preserving the mackerel had an additional benefit besides, well, preservation; it transformed the fish into something sublime, as you'll understand when you taste this classic Kyoto-style *sabazushi* ("mackerel sushi"). In this version, we share a variation where we blister the skin under the broiler to add a beautiful layer of toasty, subtle smokiness. (We tasted this version years ago along the Saba Kaido—unforgettable.) While nigiri sushi, or the Tokyo-style fingers of fish and seasoned rice that most of us think of as sushi, is 100 percent advanced knife work that we leave to the pros, sabazushi is rolled with a bamboo sushi-rolling mat, which you can achieve with a bit of practice. (But you do have to practice.)

SERVES 4

2 (6-ounce) mackerel fillets (check carefully for bones and remove any you might find)

2 tablespoons salt

¼ cup rice vinegar

SUSHI VINEGAR

3 tablespoons rice vinegar

2 tablespoons sugar

1 teaspoon salt

2 cups cooked rice, hot (see page 60)

1 tablespoon wasabi

2 tablespoons soy sauce

Generously coat both sides of the mackerel fillets with the salt, and let them cure at room temperature for 1 hour.

Lightly rinse the cured fillets under cold running water and pat them dry with paper towels. Place the fillets on a plate or in a shallow bowl and pour the rice vinegar over them. Marinate the fillets for 30 minutes, turning once.

While the fish is marinating, prepare the sushi vinegar. In a small bowl, combine the rice vinegar, sugar, and salt and whisk until the sugar is dissolved.

Transfer the rice to a bowl and pour the sushi vinegar over the top. Stir gently with a rice paddle or wide spatula, being careful

CONTINUED →

YAKI SABAZUSHI, CONTINUED

not to break the rice grains. Cover with a damp towel and let come to room temperature. (This is a critical step: If the rice is too warm, your roll may fall apart while you're cutting it.)

After the mackerel finishes curing, lightly rinse the fillets under cold running water and pat them dry with paper towels.

Preheat your broiler. Check the mackerel fillets for any bones, removing them with tweezers. When the broiler is ready, place the fillets skin-side up on a foil-lined baking sheet and broil for 1 to 2 minutes, until the skin blisters and begins to brown. Remove the fish from the broiler and let it cool completely. (Also critical, as with the rice.)

To assemble, first lay a piece of plastic wrap over a bamboo sushi mat. Place a mackerel fillet skin-side down horizontally across the mat, positioning it about halfway down. Using a knife, make a shallow cut along the centerline of the fillet from the flesh side—not completely butterflying it, but opening it slightly to create space for the rice while keeping the skin intact.

With wet hands, take half the sushi rice and form it into a log-shaped mound along the length of the mackerel. Lift the edge of the plastic wrap closest to you and bring it up and over the fish and rice, rolling forward to fully wrap, with the mackerel on top and the rice beneath. Twist the ends of the plastic wrap and fold them inside to secure the roll.

Position the wrapped roll horizontally about halfway up the bamboo mat. Lift the edge of the mat closest to you and fold it over the roll. With your fingers resting on top of the mat, press down gently to shape the roll while simultaneously stretching the opposite end of the mat away from you. This creates tension that forms a tight, compact cylinder shape. You should feel the roll becoming firm but not crushed—the rice should hold together without being compressed too tightly.

Use your sharpest knife to slice the roll. First, wipe the knife with a wet towel. Then, keeping the roll wrapped in plastic, slice it into 1-inch-thick slices. Take each piece in your hand and carefully unwrap the plastic. If the rice begins to separate, gently press it back together with your fingers. Repeat the entire process with the remaining rice and second mackerel fillet.

Arrange the pieces on four plates, making sure each person gets a mix of pieces from both the fattier belly and the tail ends of the mackerel. (The Japanese way—sharing the good stuff!) Serve with wasabi and soy sauce for dipping.

FiSH BROiLED THREE WAYS

焼き魚三種

Yaku, or cooking ingredients over direct or indirect heat, like grilling, broiling, or sautéing, is one of the five age-old foundational Japanese cooking techniques, known collectively as *goho.* (The others being simmering, steaming, frying, and cutting raw ingredients, like sashimi.) Ever since the invention of fire, it's been understood that yaku enhances the flavor of foods through caramelization and smokiness, and by developing the natural savoriness (a.k.a. umami) and sweetness of ingredients. In the following three recipes, which span super-traditional to contemporary, you'll see another key Japanese culinary concept at work, too—using seasonings to delicately enhance, but not overpower, fish. You want the natural flavors to come through, always. We're yaku-ing here with red snapper, but these techniques work perfectly with a wide variety of fish, as we'll note in the next sections.

YUAN YAKi

柚庵焼き

This is an oldie but goodie. Developed centuries ago in coastal communities to preserve fish (the original version of sushi, by the way, served the same purpose), this technique has evolved as a delicious way to marry the natural flavors of fish with traditional seasonings and tangy yuzu citrus. If you can't find yuzu juice, substitute fresh lemon juice. We also add a bit of fiery yuzu kosho (see page 28) to create another appealing flavor dimension.

SERVES 4

4 (4-ounce) boneless red snapper fillets, preferably skin on

Salt

3 tablespoons soy sauce

1 tablespoon sake

2 tablespoons mirin

1 teaspoon yuzu juice (or lemon juice)

1 teaspoon red yuzu kosho

Vegetable oil for greasing

1 lemon, cut into 4 wedges

Cut a shallow "X" into the skin of each snapper fillet to allow the marinade to penetrate from both sides.

Lightly salt the fish on both sides and let it rest at room temperature for 10 minutes to firm up the flesh. Gently wipe off any excess liquid on the surface of the fish with a paper towel.

CONTINUED →

YUAN YAKI, CONTINUED

In a small bowl, whisk together the soy sauce, sake, mirin, yuzu juice, and yuzu kosho to create the marinade. Place the red snapper fillets in a shallow dish and pour the marinade over them, ensuring each fillet is well-coated. Marinate for about 1 hour in the fridge, turning once to ensure even flavoring. Or you can marinate in the fridge overnight for a more pronounced flavor.

When you're ready to cook, preheat your broiler to high.

Line a baking sheet with aluminum foil and lightly grease it with vegetable oil to prevent sticking. Remove the snapper fillets from the marinade, gently shaking off any excess, and place them skin-side down on the prepared baking sheet.

Place the baking sheet under the preheated broiler element for 2 to 3 minutes, keeping a close eye on the fish to prevent burning. The exact time will depend on the thickness of your fillets. After 2 to 3 minutes, carefully flip the fillets and cook for 1 to 2 minutes more, or until the fish is just cooked through and lightly golden on top. Be careful not to overcook the fish.

Serve immediately with a lemon wedge on the side. Leftovers (if there are any!) can be flaked and used in onigiri (rice balls) for a delicious lunch the next day.

P.S. Yuan yaki also works great with salmon, sea bass, halibut, Spanish mackerel, and bluefish. And if you like your food spicier, add more yuzu kosho!

SHIO KOJI YAKI

塩麹焼き

Koji, Japan's "national mold" (see page 22), combined with salt begets shio koji (*shio* means "salt"), a live-culture ingredient that transforms the proteins in fish to create an incredibly tender texture and singular umami-rich flavor that we love—and you will, too. And like with the previous method, shio koji enhances but doesn't overpower the fish's beautiful natural flavor. Two more points: First, aside from creating deliciousness, shio koji offers many natural health benefits like better digestion, enhanced nutrient absorption, and improved gut health. And second, this recipe also works amazingly well with other fish like salmon, lemon sole, cod, and halibut, as well as chicken, pork, beef, and poultry. You can even mix a little shio koji with vine-ripe tomatoes for an instant, super-tasty side dish. Finally, look for shio koji in liquid puree form (bottle or tube) in the refrigerated section of Asian markets. "Liquid puree" will make sense when you see the product!

SERVES 4

4 (4-ounce) boneless red snapper fillets, preferably skin on

3 tablespoons shio koji

1 tablespoon sake

Vegetable oil for greasing

1 lemon, cut into 4 wedges

Cut a shallow "X" into the skin of each snapper fillet to allow the marinade to penetrate from both sides.

In a small bowl, mix together the shio koji and sake to create the marinade. Place the red snapper fillets in a shallow dish and pour the marinade over them, ensuring each fillet is well coated. Marinate in the fridge for at least 1 hour or up to overnight for a more intense flavor.

When you're ready to cook, preheat your broiler to high.

Line a baking sheet with aluminum foil and lightly grease it with vegetable oil to prevent sticking. Remove the red snapper fillets from the marinade, but don't wipe off the marinade—you want that flavorful coating to stay on the fish. Place skin-side up on the prepared baking sheet.

Place the baking sheet under the preheated broiler element for about 4 minutes, or until the flesh is just cooked through and opaque. Keep a close eye on the fish to prevent burning. Also, you don't need to flip the fish when cooking with shio koji. The marinade will caramelize slightly, creating a beautiful, flavor-packed crust.

Serve immediately with a wedge of lemon on the side. Any leftovers can be gently reheated and flaked over salads or used in onigiri (rice balls) for a fantastic lunch the next day.

MISO-MAYO YAKI

味噌マヨ焼き

This contemporary recipe traces its provenance to the big Japanese mayo boom of the 1980s (see page 178), blending umami-powered miso and aromatic sesame oil and paste with the whipped white stuff. Because mayo is essentially emulsified fat, for a bunch of food science reasons it helps propel the chemical transformations that happen when you *yaku* ingredients. It also helps enhance other flavors, in this case miso and sesame. But remarkably, mayo doesn't impart its own mayo-y flavor when used this way. That's key. So adding it here creates a luscious caramelized crust that broadcasts just the mouthwatering Japanese tastes while complementing but not overwhelming the fish. If you don't have sesame paste handy, just leave it out; this dish will still taste great. We're talking flexible cooking, people! Miso-mayo yaki also works great with salmon, mackerel, Chilean sea bass, and sablefish (a.k.a. black cod).

SERVES 4

4 (4-ounce) boneless red snapper fillets, preferably skin on

Salt

1 tablespoon shiro miso (see page 20)

¼ cup mayonnaise

2 teaspoons Japanese sesame paste (neri goma)

½ teaspoon toasted sesame oil

1 tablespoon Shibori Scallions (page 41), plus more for garnish

Vegetable oil for greasing

Cut a shallow "X" into the skin of each snapper fillet to allow the marinade to penetrate from both sides.

Lightly salt the fish on both sides and let it rest at room temperature for 10 minutes, to firm up the flesh. Gently wipe off any excess liquid on the surface with a paper towel.

In a small bowl, stir together the miso, mayonnaise, sesame paste, sesame oil, and 1 tablespoon scallions to create the marinade. Place the snapper fillets in a shallow dish and spread the marinade evenly over them, ensuring each fillet is well coated. Let the fish marinate at room temperature for about 15 minutes. This short marinating time allows the flavors to meld without overpowering the delicate fish.

Preheat your broiler to high.

Line a baking sheet with aluminum foil and lightly grease it with vegetable oil to prevent sticking. Transfer the marinated fillets to the prepared sheet, skin-side up, keeping as much of the marinade on the fish as possible.

When the broiler is hot, place the baking sheet about 4 inches from the heat source. Cook for 3 to 4 minutes, or until the topping is golden brown and bubbling and the flesh is just cooked through and opaque. Keep a close eye on the fish to prevent burning. The mayonnaise in the topping will help it brown beautifully.

Serve immediately, sprinkling extra scallions for freshness and color.

SAUTÉED BRANZINI WITH YUZU BROWN BUTTER

鱸柚子焦がしバター焼き

While once a foreign ingredient, butter is now about as common in modern Japanese kitchens as soy sauce. This culinary evolution traces back to the Meiji era (1868–1912), when Japan threw open its doors to Western influences faster than you can say "pass the butter, please." This recipe is a perfect example of how modern Japanese cuisine has embraced global influences while staying true to its roots. The star of the dish is the yuzu brown butter sauce. Yuzu, a Japanese citrus fruit, has a unique flavor that's somewhere between lemon, lime, and grapefruit. Its juice adds a bright, aromatic note to the nutty brown butter, while yuzu kosho adds a subtle heat and depth of flavor. Branzini is not a traditional Japanese fish, but its delicate flavor and flaky texture is perfect for this dish (and the frozen variety from stores like Costco and Trader Joe's is both easy to find and terrific). Any other mild, white-fleshed fish like sea bass or snapper will work well in this recipe, too. One final note: This is fast cooking, so have all your ingredients prepped, portioned, and ready to go before you start.

SERVES 4

4 (4-ounce) branzini fillets

½ teaspoon salt

¼ teaspoon ground white pepper

1 tablespoon olive oil

8 tablespoons (1 stick) unsalted butter, cut into 1-tablespoon pieces

2 tablespoons white wine

1 tablespoon mirin

1½ tablespoons soy sauce

1½ teaspoons red yuzu kosho

2 tablespoons yuzu juice (or lemon juice)

1 tablespoon chopped shiso leaves

FENNEL GARNISH

1 cup thinly sliced fennel

¼ teaspoon salt

1 teaspoon olive oil

½ teaspoon yuzu juice (or lemon juice)

Make a few shallow cuts to the skin of the branzini fillets, which will help it cook faster. Season the fish on both sides with the salt and white pepper, then let the fillets rest at room temperature for about 15 minutes to firm up and tenderize the flesh.

Meanwhile, prepare the fennel garnish. In a small bowl, combine the sliced fennel, salt, olive oil, and yuzu juice. Toss well and set aside to marinate.

Heat a large skillet (ideally, nonstick but any well-seasoned skillet can work) over medium-high heat. Add the olive oil and 1 tablespoon of the butter. When the butter starts to foam, add the branzini fillets skin-side down. Cook for about 2 minutes, until the skin is crispy and golden brown. Gently press down on the fish with your spatula while it cooks to help crisp up the crust. Flip the fillets and cook for another 1 to 2 minutes until the fish is just cooked through. Transfer the fish to a plate.

In the same skillet, melt the remaining butter over medium heat. Continue cooking, swirling the pan occasionally, until the butter turns golden brown and smells nutty, 3 to 4 minutes. Be careful not to let it burn.

Add the white wine, mirin, and soy sauce to the brown butter. The mixture will bubble up; this is normal. Scrape up any brown bits from the bottom of the pan and stir to combine. Simmer for about 30 seconds, then stir in the yuzu kosho and yuzu juice.

Return the fish to the skillet, spooning the sauce over the fillets. Cook for another 30 seconds to warm the fish through.

To serve, arrange the branzini fillets on a serving platter and generously spoon the yuzu brown butter sauce over them. Garnish with the fennel salad, which adds a crisp, fresh contrast, and sprinkle with chopped shiso leaves. Serve immediately.

S&B
SANSHO

SALMON TERIYAKI WITH SANSHO

鮭山椒焼き

These days teriyaki is about as ubiquitous as bagels, and it's prepared in myriad ways (some tasty, some not so much). This recipe takes a different tack, hewing to the original method first introduced over four hundred years ago when fish was marinated in sake, mirin, and soy sauce to naturally preserve it before grilling. Super practical but also savory-sweet, delicious, and beautiful to behold. (In fact, *teriyaki* is a mashup of the words for "shiny" or "lustrous" and "grill.") Bonus: This version is fast and easy to prepare in a skillet, so make sure to add it to your weeknight dinner rotation. We're using salmon but other fish make terrific teriyaki, too, such as swordfish, mahi-mahi, or even kingfish. Like other fish recipes in this section, teriyaki is quick cooking, so have all your ingredients prepped, portioned, and ready to go before you start.

SERVES 4

4 (4-ounce) salmon fillets, skin on or off

Salt

¼ cup sake

¼ cup mirin

3 tablespoons soy sauce

1 tablespoon vegetable oil

½ teaspoon sansho pepper

Lightly season the salmon fillets with salt and let them rest at room temperature for 15 minutes to remove excess moisture and tenderize. Meanwhile, prepare the teriyaki sauce by mixing the sake, mirin, and soy sauce in a small bowl; set aside. (The alcohol in the sake and mirin will cook off later.)

Heat a large skillet (ideally, nonstick but any well-seasoned skillet can work) over medium-high heat and add the oil. When the oil is hot, carefully place the salmon fillets in the pan, skin-side down if they have skin. (You can cook this in batches if it's easier.) Cook the salmon for 1 minute, then flip and cook for another 1 minute. This quick searing dries the surface of the fish, allowing it to absorb the teriyaki sauce better.

Now reduce the heat and add the teriyaki sauce to the pan. Cook for about 2 more minutes, turning the fillets once, until the sauce has reduced and becomes syrupy and glossy, like room-temperature maple syrup. As the sauce bubbles, continuously spoon it over the salmon, a basting technique that helps the sauce reduce while also flavoring and glazing the fish. The salmon should be just cooked through and moist.

Transfer the salmon to serving plates, making sure to drizzle the remaining sauce over the top. Finish each fillet with a sprinkle of sansho pepper to taste, which will add a bright citrusy and peppery kick.

HALiBUT NiTSUKE
(SIMMERED HALIBUT)
大鮃煮付け

Here's another versatile, age-old Japanese cooking technique that's a snap to whip up (maybe that's why it's age-old). *Nimono,* or simmering, is one of the five fundamental cooking techniques in Japanese cuisine (collectively called *goho*). Fish is immersed in umami-laden liquids (soy sauce, sake, mirin) and simmered to infuse flavor but not overpower the main ingredient. Apply this technique to any dense-fleshed fish for spectacular results, like striped bass, red snapper, sablefish (black cod), swordfish, mahi mahi, monkfish, or grouper. This recipe is perfect for quickly pulling together a weeknight meal. We prefer to use a large skillet here instead of a saucepan. A skillet has more surface area for the fish, and its shallow profile makes it easy to spoon the simmering liquid over fish, the last step of the cooking process.

SERVES 4

1 tablespoon thinly sliced ginger

3 tablespoons soy sauce

3 tablespoons mirin

1 tablespoon sugar

½ cup sake

¼ cup water

1 pound halibut, cut into 4 pieces (leave the skin on if it has it)

1 tablespoon finely sliced scallions

Prepare an otoshibuta (drop lid) from aluminum foil (see page 210). Set aside.

In a large skillet, combine the ginger, soy sauce, mirin, sugar, sake, and water and bring to a boil over medium heat. Give the liquid a few good stirs to fully dissolve the sugar.

Carefully lay in the halibut pieces, skin-side up (if they have skin), in the skillet. The cooking liquid doesn't have to completely cover the fish. Reduce the heat to low and place the otoshibuta directly on the halibut. Simmer the fish gently for 15 minutes, then remove the otoshibuta.

Continue simmering uncovered for 1 to 2 minutes, spooning the cooking liquid over the fish to infuse more flavor and add gloss. At this point the cooking liquid will have reduced and become syrupy.

Carefully remove the fish from the skillet and place on serving plates. (A fish spatula, longer and thinner than a regular spatula, is ideal for this task.) The fish should be very tender, so handle it gently to keep it from breaking apart.

Spoon some of the reduced cooking liquid over the fish, garnish with the scallions, and serve immediately.

MACKEREL MISO-NI
(MISO-SIMMERED MACKEREL)
鯖味噌煮

Like Halibut Nitsuke (opposite), this dish relies on one of the "big five" traditional Japanese cooking techniques—*nimono,* or simmering ingredients with naturally preserved seasonings, in this case, sake and miso. It's a super traditional dish that can also be cooked with other rich, oily fish, like Spanish mackerel, bluefish, sablefish (black cod), kingfish, or salmon. The miso deftly complements oily fish's robust flavor and infuses it with deep, beautiful umami-laden notes. It's also a snap to prepare.

SERVES 4

1 pound mackerel fillet

¼ cup sake

2 tablespoons sugar

1 cup water

2 tablespoons thinly sliced ginger

⅓ cup shiro miso (see page 20)

¼ cup thinly sliced scallions, white part only

Check for any bones in the fish and remove them (use tweezers to pull them out). Cut the fish into 4 pieces (about 4 ounces each). Score the skin of the mackerel with shallow diagonal cuts to prevent the fish from curling during cooking and to help the flesh absorb flavor. Place the fillets in a shallow bowl and pour boiling water over them. Immediately follow with cold water to stop the cooking process. This step removes any excess fishiness. Gently remove the fish and pat dry with paper towels.

Form an otoshibuta (drop lid) from aluminum foil to fit your saucepan (see page 210). Set aside.

In a shallow saucepan, combine the sake, sugar, and water. Place the mackerel pieces skin-side up in a single layer. Add the sliced ginger. Bring to a boil over high heat, then reduce the heat to medium-low. Reserve 2 tablespoons of the cooking liquid in a small bowl.

Place the otoshibuta directly on top of the fish. Simmer gently for 10 minutes without disturbing.

Meanwhile, dissolve the miso in the bowl with the reserved cooking liquid. After 10 minutes, remove the otoshibuta and pour the dissolved miso into the saucepan. Continue cooking for about 8 minutes more, occasionally spooning the sauce over the fish. The sauce will gradually reduce and become glossy, coating the fish in a beautiful glaze.

Transfer the mackerel to serving plates and spoon some of the sauce over each piece. Garnish with the sliced scallions and serve immediately.

COD KARAAGE

(FRIED COD)

鱈唐揚げ

Chicken isn't the only ingredient that gets the incomparable *karaage* ("karra-agh-eh") treatment. Fish is another delicious option. We use cod in this recipe, but white-fleshed fish like sea bass, flounder, hake, and monkfish are wonderful cooked this way, as are pollack and Spanish mackerel. Like its chicken soul-sibling (see page 211), fish karaage is marinated in mouthwatering Japanese seasonings, dredged in potato starch and rice flour for extra crisp, and deep-fried. The difference is that we fry the fish hotter and faster, so the flavor locks in but the fish stays moist and flaky. Our prediction: Once you taste this dish, you're going to have that "talk" with fish and chips.

SERVES 4

Salt for the cod, plus ½ teaspoon for the marinade

1 pound boneless cod, cut into rectangular pieces, about 1 by 2 inches

¼ cup potato starch (katakuriko)

¼ cup rice flour

2 tablespoons soy sauce

1 tablespoon mirin

1 tablespoon sake

1 teaspoon freshly grated ginger

½ teaspoon ground white pepper

Vegetable oil for frying

1 lemon, quartered

2 tablespoons chopped shiso leaves (optional)

Lightly salt the cod pieces on both sides and let them sit at room temperature for 15 minutes to draw out excess moisture and firm up the flesh. Prepare the potato starch mixture by mixing together the potato starch and rice flour on a flat plate. Set aside.

In a small bowl, combine the soy sauce, mirin, sake, grated ginger, ½ teaspoon salt, and white pepper. Add the fish to the marinade and gently stir so all the pieces are nicely coated. Let the fish marinate for 15 minutes.

When the fish is ready, gently wipe off excess marinade with a paper towel and dredge the fish in the potato starch mixture. Place the dredged pieces on a plate and repeat until all the fish is coated.

Prepare a deep-fry station. (Important: Read our note on deep-frying first, see page 213.) Fill a large cast-iron skillet with at least 1½ inches of oil, enough so that the fish will float when it cooks. Attach a deep-fry or candy thermometer to the side of the skillet and heat the oil to 330°F over medium heat. It's crucial to use a thermometer to maintain the correct temperature throughout the frying process. On a work surface near the burner, prepare a paper towel–lined plate to drain the cooked fish.

When the oil is ready, carefully add the fish, working in batches to avoid overcrowding. (Use at most half of the surface area

of the oil to cook.) Keep adjusting the heat throughout the cooking time to maintain the temperature at about 330°F. Cook for 3 to 4 minutes, turning once, until the fish is golden brown and crispy. Transfer to the paper towel–lined plate.

Serve immediately with a lemon wedge and a sprinkle of shiso leaf (if using). You want to enjoy this dish while the fish is still hot and crispy.

P.S. Instead of the shiso, another finishing option is to dust the fish with bright green aonori, flaked untoasted nori, which will add a fragrant, umami-rich taste of the sea.

7

SHELLFISH

甲殼類

Like fish, as we describe in the last chapter, shellfish also reflect the bounty of Japan's uber-rich marine ecosystem, with numerous varieties of clams, crabs, oysters, abalone, scallops, and shrimp milling about in the waters along its vast coastline. And like fish, shellfish have served as a key food source in Japan since ancient times: All you gotta do is poke around wet sand or muddy flats, and presto—you've got clam dinner! In fact, you can still witness huge prehistoric middens along the Pacific Coast (mountains of discarded shells and other ancient refuse), with one in Matsushima Bay covering almost forty acres! That's a lot of all-you-can eat.

But rooting along the coast wasn't the only way to harvest shellfish back in the day. Female divers, known as *ama,* or "women of the sea," held their breath to plunge down thirty feet or more to harvest shellfish and seaweed, a tradition stretching back some two thousand years and continuing to this day, albeit with modern diving gear replacing loincloths.

Japan's bountiful shellfish—like Miyagi, Kumamoto, and Hiroshima oysters; hamaguri and asari clams; kegani (horsehair crabs), zuwaigani (snow crabs), and taka-ashigani (spider crabs); and kuruma-ebi (tiger prawns), ama-ebi (sweet shrimp), and sakura-ebi (cherry blossom shrimp)—are prepared in myriad tasty ways, from raw to vinegared to deep-fried to dumplinged (is that a word?), recipes of which we share in the following pages.

And finally, beyond their supreme deliciousness, shellfish are keepers of deep meaning and significance in Japanese culture. Hamaguri clams, for example, symbolize harmony and marital unity due to their perfectly matching shells, and are a must-serve food at traditional wedding feasts. Shrimp signal longevity and prosperity and serve as a key ingredient in New Year's dishes to beckon a fortuitous annum. So if you're looking to make a quick buck or two, guess what you want to serve for dinner?

とりまち
素敵な大家さんだけの不動産屋
入口
中目黒
とりまち
中目黒
とりまち
釜めし
煮込み
焼鳥

OYSTERS WITH YUZU ICE

生牡蠣と柚子かき氷

Back in the aughts, Harris had an idea that he ran by Tadashi: "Maybe I can intern in your restaurant?" (at the hip Matsuri in Manhattan's Chelsea district). The response was swift: "You're gonna smell like fish and your girlfriend's gonna leave you." Hard to spin that one. But after a couple of months of (polite) nudging, Tadashi gave in. On one condition—two weeks only. Those two weeks stretched into almost two years of shifts after the day job. (It helped that Harris worked as a line cook for a spell in his twenties.) And during that time, Harris prepped and plated countless oysters for this dish, one of Matsuri's greatest hits. It's such an elegant, simple preparation; briny ocean meets bright citrus meets mouthwatering umami. If you love oysters, you'll swoon. And it's so easy to make. A few things to keep in mind: First, if you're shucking oysters for the first time, first find a relevant YouTube video for God's sake! (Harris still has the scars on his hand.) Or, just have your fishmonger do it, but make sure to eat the oysters as soon as you get home. Second, which varieties? Go west, young cook. Tadashi recommends Kumamoto, Miyagi, Kushi, or Hood Canal oysters pulled from the Pacific. These varieties tend to be smaller and sweeter, not brine bombs like their Atlantic cousins.

SERVES 4

YUZU ICE

1 cup yuzu juice (or lemon or lime juice)

¼ cup dashi (see page 40), cooled

2 tablespoons mirin, brought to boil and cooled

3 tablespoons usukuchi soy sauce

FOR SERVING

12 fresh oysters (Kumamoto preferred)

2 teaspoons finely chopped chives

1 teaspoon red yuzu kosho

Make the yuzu ice at least 4 hours before serving. In a wide, shallow container, combine the yuzu juice, dashi, mirin, and usukuchi soy sauce. The container should allow the liquid to spread about 1 inch deep. Cover and freeze until solid, about 4 hours.

When ready to serve, use a dinner fork to scrape the frozen mixture, creating light, fluffy crystals. The texture should resemble fresh snow; if it's too solid to scrape, let it stand at room temperature for 2 to 3 minutes.

Have your oysters shucked as close to serving time as possible. If shucking them yourself, keep them very cold and layered on ice until ready to plate. We like to serve the oysters on a big platter. Arrange on the platter, nestled atop a mori shio (a small mound of moistened salt), if you desire. Top each oyster with 1 tablespoon of shaved ice, sprinkle with a pinch of chopped chives, and crown with a small dab of yuzu kosho, about the size of a peppercorn. Use chopsticks to achieve this. Serve immediately before the ice melts.

KANi SHUMAi

蟹しゅうまい

It's not every day that a dumpling receives a "Contribution to the City" award, but that's exactly what happened in Yokohama with shumai. A seaside city just outside Tokyo with a bustling port, Yokohama has long been a gateway for goods, foods, and people arriving from afar, including *sui mai,* Chinese dim sum dumplings that came with Chinese immigrants to the port over a century ago and were quickly adopted as *shumai* in Japan. In fact, a company called Kiyoken began pumping out these little bites of joy en masse in the 1920s, employing "shumai girls" clad in red Chinese-style outfits to hawk them at train stations. They didn't have to sell too hard: Delicious steamed or fried, hot or at room temp, the open-topped dumplings quickly became a culinary hit across the country. In fact, the still-thriving Kiyoken produces some 800,000 shumai daily at their Yokohama factory today, hence the urban award. And another surprise on this dumpling journey: Home cooks discovered how easy—and fun—it is to make shumai themselves, as you'll see when you conjure up your own batch. Shumai can be prepared with pork, shrimp, or a combo of the two, as well as with other ingredients. Here we offer a version with crab (*kani*) that we love. Final note: Shumai freeze beautifully, so fold a ton of 'em! Place uncooked shumai on a baking sheet lined with parchment paper, freeze until solid, then transfer them to a freezer bag. Cook directly from frozen, adding an extra minute or two to the cooking time.

MAKES 24 DUMPLINGS

FILLING

½ pound shrimp, peeled and deveined (a white fish such as cod will work, too)

1 cup crabmeat

¼ cup finely chopped red onion (for subtle flavor and nice color, but white or yellow onion works, too)

1 tablespoon finely chopped ginger

1 tablespoon mayonnaise

1 tablespoon mirin

2 teaspoons soy sauce

2 tablespoons potato starch (katakuriko), plus extra for dusting

24 squares shumai wrappers (wonton wrappers work, too)

FOR SERVING

½ teaspoon sesame oil (if pan-frying)

2 tablespoons soy sauce

2 teaspoons karashi mustard (or tobanjan or yuzu kosho, if you prefer)

Place the shrimp in a food processor and pulse very briefly, 5 to 10 seconds. The key here is to achieve a coarse mince, where you can still see small pieces, not a smooth paste. You want texture in your final dumpling. If you don't have a food processor, finely chop the shrimp with a knife. If using white fish instead of shrimp, process it the same way.

In a large bowl, combine the shrimp, crabmeat, onion, ginger, mayonnaise, mirin, soy sauce, and potato starch. Mix with your hands until everything is well combined and the mixture becomes slightly sticky—using your hands helps you feel when the texture is right. The mayonnaise helps bind the mixture while adding richness and flavor.

To form the shumai, take one wrapper and place it in the palm of your left hand (if right-handed). Place 1 tablespoon of filling in the center—being precise with this measurement helps ensure even cooking.

CONTINUED →

HOW TO FORM SHUMAI

KANi SHUMAi, CONTINUED

Now comes the distinctive shumai-forming technique: Create a ring with your index finger and thumb, like making an "OK" sign. Place the wrapper with filling into this ring, then use your thumb to gently press down on the top edge while your other fingers support the bottom. Begin rotating the dumpling in place with your "ring" thumb and index finger, turning it in a circular motion. As you rotate, press and guide the wrapper edges upward, working your way around to create a cylindrical shape. The wrapper will naturally form pleats as you rotate and tighten. Don't press too tight, but firm enough that the dumpling holds its shape. The filling should remain visible at the top. The final shape should look like a little basket with the filling slightly below the wrapper's edge. Shumai wrappers are very delicate, so handle them gently to avoid tearing. Place the prepared shumai on a plate dusted with potato starch, and continue until all are wrapped. Forming shumai takes a little practice so don't sweat it if the first dumplings look like something out of *Alien*!

Now, two choices for cooking: steaming, the traditional way, or pan-frying, which is also fantastic.

For steaming, set up a steamer in a large pot. Line your steamer with parchment paper, poking several holes in it for the steam to come through. Add enough water for steaming, cover, and bring the pot to a boil over medium heat. Arrange the shumai in the steamer, leaving space around each dumpling as they will expand slightly. Steam over the boiling water for about 6 minutes, until the shumai are cooked through. Repeat with more shumai.

To pan-fry, heat a nonstick or well-seasoned cast-iron skillet over medium heat. Add ½ teaspoon sesame oil—just enough to barely coat the bottom of the pan. Place the shumai in the pan and cook for about 30 seconds until they start to brown on the bottom. Add ½ cup water, cover immediately, and cook for about 3 minutes. Uncover and continue cooking for 1 minute more until the water evaporates and the bottoms are crispy. (This technique is similar to cooking gyoza, see page 246.)

Combine the soy sauce and karashi mustard in small dishes for dipping. You can also substitute tobanjan or yuzu kosho for the karashi mustard, if you desire.

Let the shumai cool for a minute or two before serving; if they're super hot you won't taste all the flavors (and you'll burn the roof of your mouth). Serve with the dipping sauce on the side.

LITTLENECK CLAMS WITH MISO BUTTER

蛤味噌バター蒸し

Miso and butter, and soy sauce and butter are two aha flavor moments Japanese cooks discovered as they incorporated more and more Western ingredients into their cooking. With miso, its deep umami and salt meet the richness of butter in a mind-blowing flavor synergy. This combo is super versatile, and is even used in cookies and cakes. Here we apply the miso butter treatment to clams, which add their own briny deliciousness. This recipe is fast and easy to prepare. Use littleneck or Manila clams, which are more tender than cherrystone or other varieties. (Manila clams, called *asari* in Japan, are often sold in Asian markets; if you can find them, use 'em; they have an incredible, beautiful clam flavor.) This method also works wonderfully with mussels.

SERVES 4

Kosher or sea salt

24 littleneck or Manila clams

Salt

3 tablespoons butter

2 teaspoons finely chopped garlic

½ teaspoon dried Japanese red chile pepper flakes (red pepper flakes will work, too)

½ cup sake

1 tablespoon Sendai miso (or other aka miso)

1 tablespoon chopped scallions

At least two hours before cooking or overnight, soak the clams in a large bowl of salted water. Use 1 teaspoon kosher or sea salt (but not iodized salt) per 1 cup cold water. Whisk to dissolve the salt, add the clams, and keep the bowl in the refrigerator. Rinse the clams before cooking them. This process prompts the clams to spit out any sand in their shells (you don't want grit when you bite into your clams).

In a large saucepan over medium heat, melt the butter. Add the garlic and dried chile flakes and cook, stirring frequently, for about 30 seconds, until the garlic becomes fragrant but doesn't brown and the butter begins to foam.

Add the clams and stir for a few seconds to coat with the butter mixture. Pour in the sake, increase the heat to medium-high, and cover the pan. Cook for 3 to 5 minutes, until the clams begin to open.

Transfer the opened clams to a serving bowl, leaving the cooking liquid in the pan. (Discard any clams that do not open.) Return the pan to medium heat and whisk in the miso until it completely dissolves into the sauce and becomes smooth, about 30 seconds. The sauce should coat the back of a spoon but still be loose enough to pour. If it's too thick, add a splash of water.

Pour the miso-butter sauce over the clams and garnish with the chopped scallions. Serve immediately.

EBi iTAME

海老炒め

Here's an easy and satisfying dish you can munch on in minutes. *Itame* means "quick stir-frying." The olive oil here contributes beautiful flavor as well as a contemporary flourish, while sake, soy sauce, shiso, and aromatics give the dish its quintessential Japanese character. The sum of all these particular parts is pure deliciousness, without a ton of effort. Pair these sautéed shrimp with stir-fried vegetables (see page 135) and the reheated cooked rice you're storing in the freezer (see page 58, you're doing this, right?), and presto—instant weeknight meal for the gang. Keep in mind that for a dish that cooks this quickly, under four minutes, it's critical to prep all your ingredients before you get busy at the burner.

SERVES 4

1 pound (16 to 20 pieces) large shrimp, peeled

¼ teaspoon salt, plus extra for seasoning the shrimp

1 tablespoon sake

1 tablespoon soy sauce

1 tablespoon finely chopped garlic

½ teaspoon dried Japanese red chile pepper flakes (red pepper flakes will work, too)

2 teaspoons finely chopped shiso (or use cilantro or parsley)

2 tablespoons olive oil

Devein the shrimp by making a shallow cut along the back of each shrimp and scraping out the digestive tract (a.k.a. the vein). This process also butterflies the shrimp, creating more surface area to absorb the sauce. Season with salt and set aside.

In a small bowl, combine the ¼ teaspoon salt, sake, and soy sauce. Make sure your chopped garlic, dried chile flakes, and shiso are within easy reach of the stove.

Preheat a large skillet over medium-high heat. Add the olive oil and let it heat until it starts smoking. Add the shrimp in a single layer and cook for 1 minute. Use tongs to flip the shrimp and cook for 1 minute more. Add the garlic and chile flakes and cook for 30 seconds, stirring constantly to release their fragrance but being careful not to burn the garlic.

Pour in the sake and soy sauce mixture and keep stirring until most of the liquid evaporates, about 1 minute. (You're not creating a sauce with this dish.) Mix in the shiso, turn off the heat, and transfer to a large platter. Serve immediately.

EBI MAYO

(FRIED SHRIMP WITH MAYO SAUCE)

海老マヨ

Mayonnaise, how we love thee. In a homogeneous country like Japan, cultural phenomena sweep across the country almost instantly—known as *boomu,* or a boom. Now with social media, this is a given. But back in the 1980s before all that digital noise, mayonnaise suddenly became the "it" ingredient almost overnight. And ebi mayo, which emerged from restaurants before being quickly adopted by home cooks, rose to the top. In this dish, crispy fried shrimp meets a velvety, tangy sauce—need we say more? If you can find Japanese mayo like Kewpie, use it. It's richer and more flavorful than Hellmann's and the like because it uses only egg yolks and robust rice vinegar. Interestingly, Kewpie was first introduced in 1925 by founder Toichiro Nakashima in the hope of "improving the physique of Japanese people." So if you start to get shredded after a few servings of ebi mayo . . . well, you're welcome!

SERVES 4

MAYO SAUCE

½ cup Japanese mayonnaise

1 egg yolk

1 tablespoon plain yogurt

2 teaspoons ketchup

1 teaspoon red yuzu kosho

1 teaspoon sugar

½ teaspoon salt

SHRIMP

1 pound (16 to 20 pieces) large shrimp, peeled

1 egg white

½ teaspoon salt

¼ teaspoon ground white pepper

1 teaspoon sake

Vegetable oil for frying

3 tablespoons potato starch (katakuriko)

FOR SERVING

4 Boston lettuce leaves

2 tablespoons finely sliced scallions

Prepare the mayo sauce. In a microwave-safe bowl, whisk together all sauce ingredients until smooth. Microwave for 30 seconds, then stir. Microwave for another 30 seconds and stir again. You'll see ribbons in the sauce as you stir, which means that it's ready. Transfer to a bowl and set aside to come to room temperature. This process firms up the sauce, giving it a richer texture and flavor.

(If you don't have a microwave, you can use a double boiler: Place the bowl with the sauce ingredients over a pot of simmering water and stir constantly for about 2 minutes, until the sauce is warm and slightly thickened and ribbons appear when you stir. Remove from the heat and let it cool.)

For the shrimp, remove tails and devein if necessary (see page 177). Blot the shrimp dry with a paper towel to remove moisture, which will help them fry crispier. In a medium bowl, combine the shrimp with the egg white, salt, white pepper, and sake. Using your hands, mix vigorously for about 60 seconds until the egg white becomes foamy. This creates tiny air bubbles in the egg white, which will result in a lighter, lacier coating when fried (think tempura).

CONTINUED →

EBi MAYO, CONTINUED

Prepare a deep-fry station. (Important: Read our note on deep-frying first, see page 213.) Fill a large cast-iron skillet or heavy-bottomed pot with 2 inches of oil, enough so that the shrimp will float during frying. Attach a deep-fry or candy thermometer to the side of the skillet and heat the oil to 350°F over medium heat. It's crucial to use a thermometer to maintain the correct temperature throughout the frying process. While the oil is heating, lightly dredge the shrimp in the potato starch, shaking off any excess. Do this step right before frying, not ahead of time, so the coating doesn't get soggy. On a work surface near the burner, prepare a paper towel–lined plate to drain the cooked shrimp.

When the oil is ready, fry the shrimp for about 1 minute on each side, until light tan-colored and crispy. The shrimp doesn't need to be completely covered by the oil. After adding the shrimp, increase the heat slightly to maintain the oil temperature (check your thermometer). Be careful not to overcook the shrimp. You can fry the shrimp in batches if it's easier. Drain the fried shrimp on the prepared plate.

To serve, arrange a lettuce leaf on each plate. In the bowl of mayo sauce, gently toss the hot fried shrimp until coated with all the sauce. Place the shrimp on the lettuce leaves, sprinkle with sliced scallions, and serve immediately while the shrimp are still crispy.

You can also serve this dish with the mayo sauce on the side for dipping, if you'd like, but coating the shrimp is the typical way this dish is served in Japan.

MONJAYAKI

もんじゃ焼き

Monjayaki, or simply, monja, is *Shitamachi* soul food. Literally "the town below the castle," Shitamachi is the blue-collar section of Tokyo that for centuries housed the city's artisans, fishermen, and traditional food producers, an area that developed its own brassy subculture, dialect, sense of cool (called *iki*), and of course, favorite grub. Monja, with roots going back to the 1600s, is one of this area's most popular dishes. A loose, savory pancake with the consistency of melted cheddar, it's made by mixing a watery batter of flour, water, Worcestershire, and cabbage with other ingredients, and sizzled on a flat-top griddle. The result is crispy, toasty, gooey, fun—and delicious. In fact, today there's even a "Monja Street" (Nishinaka Dori in Shitamachi) lined with at least fifty monja restaurants packed with diners arrayed around cast-iron griddles, going to town with chopsticks and signature stainless steel mini-spatulas. For Tadashi, Shitamachi boy that he is, monja is personal. As a wee lad, his home was next door to a *dagashiya,* or traditional snack shop, where the owner lived in the rear of the store. Tadashi would pop into the shop for *amanato,* sweet dried black beans, and one-penny *sembei,* rice crackers. The owner also had an electric griddle fired up in her living area where the aroma of sizzling monja beckoned customers, and adorable, kindergarten-aged Tadashi would often find himself sitting cross-legged back there, mini-spatula in hand. This recipe is adapted for a skillet (nonstick or ceramic-coated are ideal), but you eat the same way you would in Shitamachi, mini-spatula or not: Everyone piles around one big monja pancake and digs in. This recipe also employs cake flour, which is less glutinous than regular flour, producing a lighter texture.

SERVES 4, AS A SHARED DISH

⅓ cup cake flour

3 tablespoons Worcestershire sauce

1 tablespoon soy sauce

½ teaspoon tobanjan

1 cup thinly sliced green cabbage (see Note on page 106)

¼ cup dried baby shrimp (sakura ebi)

½ cup roughly chopped squid (about 6 ounces)

1 tablespoon sesame oil

2 teaspoons aonori (powdered seaweed)

In a large bowl, combine the cake flour, Worcestershire sauce, soy sauce, tobanjan, and 2 cups of water. Whisk together until smooth. The mixture will be very watery—so watery you might think it's wrong, but this is exactly what you want. Add the cabbage, dried baby shrimp, and chopped squid to the bowl. Stir well to combine.

Heat a large skillet over medium-low heat. Add the sesame oil and spread it evenly across the cooking surface with a paper towel. The skillet should be thoroughly preheated to prevent sticking, though some sticking is part of the charm of this dish.

CONTINUED →

MONJAYAKI, CONTINUED

Using a slotted spoon—it is important to leave most of the liquid behind—transfer the solid ingredients (cabbage, shrimp, and squid) to the skillet. Spread the ingredients out and cook, stirring constantly for about 1 minute until the cabbage begins to soften.

Pour the remaining liquid mixture over the solid ingredients. Keep stirring as the liquid comes to a boil and scrape up any bits that stick to the bottom of the pan. Cook, stirring frequently, until the mixture begins to thicken and become sticky, similar to the consistency of thick oatmeal, about 5 minutes. Don't worry if it sticks—the caramelized bits that you scrape up add flavor and are part of the authentic monja experience. Once the mixture has thickened and is bubbling steadily, let it cook for 1 to 2 minutes more, until the edges start to get a bit crispy. Scrape these crispy bits back into the mixture.

Transfer the monja to a large serving platter and sprinkle the aonori over the top. Don't worry about the presentation; this isn't haute cuisine. Gather everyone around the platter and hand them dinner spoons (mini-spatula stand-ins) and enjoy it together while it's hot.

P.S. Other ingredients you can add to monja include pork, beef, chicken, oysters, scallops, clams, or even cheese (like cheddar).

VINEGAR-CURED SCALLOPS

帆立貝酢締め

Vinegared seafood is the kissing cousin of sushi: it's raw like sushi, sliced like sushi, and *nama* like sushi—*nama,* or preparing raw ingredients, being one of the five fundamental Japanese cooking methods (we talk more about this on page 15). But unlike sushi, which is specialized chef cooking, vinegaring is achievable home fare that yields spectacular results. Like in this recipe, whose roots stretch back to the seventeenth century when vinegar was used to naturally preserve seafood. Here the rice vinegar infuses scallops with acidity and delicate sweetness and firms up their exterior, which allows them to absorb flavors like tangy ume paste, wasabi, and olive oil (flashing forward now to the twenty-first century). Try this recipe, too, with a white-fleshed fish like fluke or sea bass or with bay scallops or fresh raw shrimp (if you're using frozen shrimp, use it right away).

SERVES 4

¼ teaspoon salt

4 large sea scallops (about 6 ounces total)

¼ cup rice vinegar

2 tablespoons sake

2 teaspoons mirin

1 tablespoon ume paste

½ teaspoon wasabi

1 teaspoon olive oil

¼ cup thinly sliced red onion

1 small Persian cucumber, thinly sliced into rounds

4 shiso leaves, roughly chopped

Lightly salt the scallops and let them rest in a small bowl for 5 minutes to concentrate their flavor and release moisture. When they're ready, gently wipe off the moisture from the surface of the scallops with a paper towel and pour the rice vinegar over them, making sure each scallop is fully submerged. The vinegar will start to "cook" the scallops. Let them cure for 15 minutes, turning them once halfway through. You'll notice the scallops gradually becoming more opaque and slightly firmer to the touch.

In a small saucepan, bring the sake and mirin to a boil over medium heat to evaporate the alcohol (a process called *iri sake*). Immediately remove from the heat and let the mixture cool to room temperature. When cool, whisk in the ume paste, wasabi, and olive oil until well combined. The sauce should have a smooth consistency and a beautiful pink hue.

When the scallops are ready, remove them from the vinegar and thinly slice them. In a medium bowl, combine the scallops, red onion, and cucumber. Pour the ume sauce over them and gently toss to coat everything evenly.

To serve, divide the scallop mixture among four small plates or shallow bowls. Sprinkle the chopped shiso leaves over and serve.

8

EGGS, CHICKEN, AND DUCK

卵、鶏、鴨

You can thank Arkansas for Japan's love affair with chicken. During the US occupation of Japan after World War II, the country adopted production methods for broiler chickens pioneered by Tyson Foods and other leading Arkansas poultry companies, which helped stave off food shortages, especially of protein. (Broilers are fast-growing chickens bred for meat; they're what you buy in the supermarket.) Within a few years, output surged, the price of chicken plummeted, and its popularity exploded; today, chicken is Japan's most popular meat, consumed more than either pork or beef.

Once chicken flew the coop, as it were, cooks quickly embraced this ingredient. And why not? Fermented Japanese seasonings like soy sauce and miso marry beautifully with chicken's natural flavors, teasing out the bird's intrinsic umami. Moreover, the fermented complexity enhances chicken's delicious richness without overpowering it. Sake helps tenderize chicken meat, while aromatics like ginger and garlic are classic pairings that cut through the fat and boost savoriness. You'll experience all this in beloved dishes like chikuzen-ni, karaage, tori nanban sandwiches, and, of course, wings, all of which we share in the recipes that follow.

And we'd be remiss if we didn't mention a newish Japanese Christmas treat—Kentucky Fried Chicken's "Party Barrel." In the 1970s, KFC launched a "Kentucky for Christmas" ad campaign in Japan, where the holiday is marked as a secular celebration. The idea took root and became an unlikely Christmas tradition there, with December 24 being KFC's busiest day of the year in Japan.

Eggs were once considered elite eats and also used medicinally because of their nutritional value. But by the 1800s, eggs went mainstream and became symbols of modern nutrition. Today, eggs are central to the Japanese diet, and beloved: Japanese consume the second highest number of eggs per capita in the world. And because of Japan's culture of food safety, eating eggs lightly cooked or raw is very common, like with our Runny Egg Omelet (page 189), and Tamago Kake Gohan a.k.a. "TKG" (page 63).

Not to be forgotten, ducks, which are native to Japan, got a pass for some reason from the aforementioned Emperor Tenmu's meat ban in the 600s, so they've been hunted and cultivated throughout the country's history. We share a couple of tasty duck recipes here, including the traditional (and delicious) *jibuni,* a variety of duck stew, and duck wontons . . . 'cause we're kinda dumpling crazed!

JIDORI, JAPANESE HEIRLOOM CHICKEN

Japanese chicken isn't all broilers all the time. Different regions of the country proudly boast their own bespoke heirloom breeds that can go toe-to-toe with France's famed Bresse Gauloise birds in terms of heavenly chicken-y flavor and texture. Japan's heirloom breeds are called *jidori,* a term that translates to "chicken of the earth." While their origins stretch back more than two thousand years with the introduction of chickens from China, by the late nineteenth century Japan had established thirty-eight indigenous chicken breeds, which are the precursors of modern jidori lineages.

Today, only 1 percent of Japanese chicken is considered jidori, with the "Three Great Jidori" of Japan being Nagoya Cochin from central Japan, Satsuma jidori from the country's Deep South, and Hinai jidori from Tohoku, in Japan's far north. Hinai jidori, interestingly, traces its roots back four hundred years and were so prized they were once used as tax payments and have been awarded a national designation.

Harris, by the way, once happened upon a Hinai jidori farmer in rural Akita Prefecture who was serenading his flock with strains of Mozart pumped out of massive speakers to, in his words, "make them happy." If you love your birds, they'll love you back.

Jidori are free-range, eat a natural diet, and are reared for twice as long as broilers. Mozart or not, all the tender loving care bestowed on jidori produces firmer meat and deep umami-laden flavor and deliciousness, so good that jidori is sometimes served as *torisashi,* chicken sashimi (which is amazing, trust us).

RUNNY EGG OMELET

トロトロオムレツ

In France there's a saying that the first omelet goes to the dog. Same goes for this Japanese version. You'll have to practice a bit to get a handle on cooking this omelet, but it's worth it! And here's why. *Torotoro tamago,* as it's known in Japan, is a testament to the beautiful simplicity of Japanese cuisine. Unlike diner-style omelets that are usually loaded with fillings, this version celebrates the pure, rich flavor of eggs. The technique results in an omelet that's golden and set on the outside, but with a lusciously creamy, almost custard-like center. The key to nailing this omelet is temperature control and timing. You want to cook it over low heat so it just sets, but the inside stays delightfully runny. We pair this omelet with a homemade demi-glace sauce, a favorite combination in Japan. Demi-glace is now considered fuddy-duddy cooking in France and almost forgotten, but it's an early-twentieth-century import to Japan that's still popular there to this day. A runny egg omelet with demi-glace sauce is often served over rice, which becomes a complete meal. Cook each omelet one at a time, and use a good-quality nonstick pan and a rubber or silicone spatula. Okay, give it a go. Fido is waiting!

MAKES 1 OMELET

3 large eggs

1 tablespoon milk

¼ teaspoon salt

Pinch of ground white pepper

1 tablespoon butter

Demi-Glace Sauce (recipe follows)

In a bowl, gently beat the eggs, milk, salt, and white pepper. Don't overmix—you want to see distinct streaks of white and yolk in the mixture. This will help create an interesting texture in the final omelet.

Place an 8-inch nonstick skillet over medium-low heat (do not preheat). Add the butter and let it melt, tilting the pan to coat the entire surface. When the butter starts to foam but before it browns, pour in the egg mixture.

As the eggs begin to set at the edges, use a rubber or silicone spatula to gently push the cooked portions toward the center of the pan. Tilt the pan to allow the uncooked egg to flow into the empty spaces. Skim the edges with your spatula to keep them from sticking. Gently swirl the eggs in a circular motion to cook them. Repeat this process until the omelet is set on the bottom but still wet and creamy on top, after about 2 minutes.

CONTINUED →

HOW TO COOK RUNNY EGG OMELET

RUNNY EGG OMELET, CONTINUED

Now it's time to shape the omelet. (You'll know it's ready for the next step when the egg doesn't move much when you shake the pan, more jiggly than runny.) Decrease the heat to low. Using your spatula, fold one-third of the omelet over toward the center. Then, fold the opposite side over to create an elongated, trifold shape that looks like a giant almond.

Let it cook for another 30 seconds. Now carefully flip the omelet so the seam side is down so it can seal. Turn off the heat. The residual heat from the pan will continue to cook the eggs slightly.

To serve, carefully slide the omelet onto a plate or over rice, seam-side down. The exterior should be a pale golden color, while the interior remains soft and creamy. Make a small incision lengthwise on top to reveal the runny interior—this is particularly visually appealing when serving. Pour a ribbon of demi-glace over the omelet and serve immediately.

DEMI-GLACE SAUCE

デミグラスソース

Arriving in the late nineteenth century when Western cooking was new and exciting and all the rage, this classic French sauce has been adopted into many popular *yoshoku* (Western-influenced) dishes in Japan and is loved to this day. Demi-glace is a rich, intensely flavored brown sauce traditionally made by reducing beef stock, wine, aromatics, and tomato puree. In Japan, soy sauce and mirin are also added to give it the cuisine's signature umami boost. Demi-glace serves to complement dishes like *hamburg,* the Japanese version of a hamburger, and a runny egg omelet. While packaged Japanese demi-glace sauce is readily available, we urge you to make it at home. Demi-glace will keep in the freezer for up to three months, so you can enjoy this sauce again and again.

MAKES ABOUT 2 CUPS

1 tablespoon butter

1 medium onion (about ½ pound), thinly sliced

1 stalk celery, chopped

1 small carrot, chopped

2 garlic cloves, chopped

1 cup red wine

4 cups low-sodium beef stock

¼ cup mirin

½ cup tomato puree

2 tablespoons soy sauce

In a large heavy-bottomed pot, melt the butter over medium-low heat. Add the sliced onions and cook, stirring occasionally, 15 to 20 minutes. You're looking for the onions to caramelize slowly, developing a deep, golden color and sweet flavor. This process is crucial for building the sauce's rich base, so be patient and resist the urge to rush it.

Once the onions are beautifully caramelized, increase the heat to medium-low and add the celery, carrot, and garlic. Cook for another 5 minutes, stirring frequently, until the vegetables have softened and are fragrant.

Increase the heat to medium-high and add the red wine. Let it bubble vigorously for about 5 minutes, stirring occasionally and scraping the bottom of the pot to release any browned bits.

Pour in the stock, mirin, and tomato puree. Bring the mixture to a boil, then reduce the heat to maintain a gentle simmer. Cook, stirring occasionally, for 1 hour. The liquid should reduce by about half, becoming darker and concentrated.

Add the soy sauce, mix together, and turn off the heat. The sauce should now be thick enough to coat the back of a spoon.

Allow the sauce to come to room temperature. Now blend it in batches in a blender, pulsing for about 30 seconds until mostly smooth. After blending, you can strain it through a fine-mesh sieve to create a more velvety sauce, but this step is optional.

Reheat the sauce before serving. It may darken slightly, but that won't affect the flavor. If the sauce becomes too thick when reheated, thin it out with a little beef stock or water.

ATSUYAKi TAMAGO

(TOKYO-STYLE ROLLED OMELET)

厚焼き玉子

Many of us are familiar with *dashimaki,* or the dashi rolled omelet, a sushi bar staple. Eggs are scrambled with dashi stock and cooked and rolled in thin layers in special rectangular pans to create a signature log shape, a cooking technique closely identified with Kyoto. The eggs we cook here are a variation that hails from Tokyo called *atsuyaki* ("thick cooked"), the omelets that Tokyo-dude Tadashi grew up with. While Japanese regional cooking might not be so familiar outside the country, there are big differences in dialect, attitudes, and cooking styles between the West (Kyoto area, called the Kansai region) and the East (Tokyo area, called the Kanto region). You can see these distinctions expressed in this humble omelet, which in Tokyo dispenses with dashi and accentuates the natural sweetness of eggs with a bit of sugar. And because there's no dashi cutting the egg mixture, the Tokyo version is denser (hence, "thick") and the edges may be caramelized a bit, which adds another delightful note. And guess what? You can easily knock this omelet out with a nonstick skillet (we use an 8-inch size) and a rubber spatula (a must). You will have to practice a bit to get the technique down, but you'll get the hang of it before you blow through a carton of eggs. We believe in you.

MAKES 1 OMELET

3 eggs

2 teaspoons sugar

1 tablespoon soy sauce

½ teaspoon sesame oil

2 tablespoons grated daikon (daikon oroshi, optional)

In a bowl, whisk together the eggs, sugar, and soy sauce until well combined and the sugar has dissolved.

Heat a medium nonstick skillet over medium heat. Add the sesame oil, and use a paper towel to lightly coat the skillet. (Save the oil-soaked paper towel on a small dish next to the stove; you'll use it again.) You don't want to add too much oil; the skillet should look pretty dry.

Reduce the heat to medium-low and pour about one-third of the egg mixture into the skillet, tilting to cover the bottom evenly. When the egg is mostly set but still slightly wet on top, after about 30 seconds, start rolling it from one end of the skillet to the other using your rubber spatula. The egg should be as thin as a crepe when you start rolling.

CONTINUED →

ATSUYAKI TAMAGO, CONTINUED

Wipe the pan with the paper towel to coat the skillet with a little more oil, and add another third of the egg mixture. Lift the rolled portion to let the raw egg flow underneath. Tilt the pan to coat the bottom and cook the egg evenly. When the egg is mostly set but still slightly wet on top (the wet egg will act as "glue" to hold the rolled omelet shape), after about 30 seconds, start rolling again but this time in the opposite direction, starting with the previously rolled portion until you get to the other end of the skillet.

Now wipe the pan with the oil-saturated paper towel and pour in the rest of the egg mixture. Lift the rolled portion to let the raw egg flow underneath, and tilt the pan to coat the bottom. Cook the remaining egg evenly, about 30 seconds. Roll again, starting with the previously rolled portion, to roll up the rest of the egg (see Note).

At this point you'll have a nice, thick, layered omelet in the skillet. Cook for 1 minute. Carefully flip the omelet to cook the other side, and press it against the side of the skillet to shape it into a half-moon. If the omelet breaks apart a bit when flipping, don't despair, just use your rubber spatula to push it back together. Cook for 1 more minute to allow the inside of the egg to cook through.

Remove the omelet from the pan and slice into four pieces. Serve immediately, with a mound of grated daikon if you'd like, to add a fresh contrast and cut the richness of the egg (see page 133).

NOTE

Depending on the size of your skillet, you may have to repeat the rolling process until you incorporate all your egg, but that's fine.

ATSUYAKI TAMAGO SANDO

Hold on, we're not done with atsuyaki tamago just yet. This omelet makes an awesome—and beloved in Tokyo, naturally—egg sandwich (*sando*). Just toast two slices of Japanese milk bread (see page 235) or any white bread, trim the crusts, and slide the egg between them. Cut the sandwich into quarters and go to town or pack it as a lunch you'll swoon over.

HOW TO COOK ATSUYAKI TAMAGO

CHICKEN MISO GYOZA

鶏味噌餃子

This gyoza is a chicken, shiitake, and miso umami bomb. The recipe calls for boiling the gyoza to give you another cooking option, which is the original Chinese preparation style and yields lovely, juicy dumplings. It works particularly well with homemade gyoza skins (see page 201), which tend to be a little thicker than store-bought, adding another dimension of chewy texture. But if you prefer them yaki-gyoza style, that is, frying-and-steaming these puppies, we're cool with that (also super delicious, see page 247). There's a lot of chopping in this recipe so if you have a food processor and you're so inclined, don't hesitate to use it here.

MAKES ABOUT 24 GYOZA

3 dried shiitake mushrooms

2 cups finely chopped cabbage (you can do this with a food processor)

½ teaspoon salt, plus more for seasoning

2 tablespoons soy sauce

2 tablespoons rice vinegar

Rayu chili oil to taste

½ pound boneless, skinless chicken thighs

¼ cup thinly sliced scallions

¼ cup finely chopped shiso

1 teaspoon finely chopped garlic

1 teaspoon finely chopped ginger

1 tablespoon shiro miso (see page 20)

1 tablespoon sake

2 teaspoons sesame oil

½ teaspoon tobanjan

¼ teaspoon ground white pepper

1 tablespoon potato starch (katakuriko)

3 tablespoons warm water

24 gyoza skins (store-bought or homemade, recipe follows)

Combine the shiitake in a bowl with enough hot water to cover. Let soak for 30 minutes, until fully softened. Drain (discard the water). Remove the stems, squeeze out any excess liquid, and finely chop the caps. Set aside.

Place the cabbage in a large bowl and sprinkle with the ½ teaspoon salt. Mix well with your hands, really massaging the salt into the cabbage until it starts to soften and release liquid. Let sit for 10 minutes. Transfer the cabbage to a clean kitchen towel, gather the corners together, and twist tightly over the sink, squeezing out as much liquid as possible. Keep twisting and squeezing until no more water drips out. This step is crucial for preventing soggy gyoza.

In a small bowl, whisk together the soy sauce and rice vinegar with a touch of rayu chili oil to create a classic dipping sauce. Set aside. (Substituting a dab of citrusy red yuzu kosho for the rayu is also fantastic.)

Cut the chicken thighs into 1-inch pieces. In a food processor, pulse the chicken pieces until coarsely ground. Watch carefully as you pulse; the texture can go from perfect to too fine in just one or two pulses. The meat should be evenly chopped but still have some texture and should look roughly ground, not pasty or pureed.

CONTINUED →

CHICKEN MISO GYOZA, CONTINUED

In a large bowl, combine the squeezed cabbage, ground chicken, shiitakes, scallions, shiso, garlic, ginger, miso, sake, sesame oil, tobanjan, and white pepper. Using your hands, mix and squeeze the ingredients together for about 2 minutes. You want to really work the mixture until it becomes sticky and holds together when pressed. The texture should be cohesive but still show distinct pieces of cabbage. When you pick up a small amount, it should hold together in a clump.

In a small bowl, whisk the potato starch with the warm water. This is the "glue" for sealing the gyoza.

To fold the gyoza, hold a skin in the palm of one hand with the floured-side down. Moisten the entire edge with the potato starch mixture. Place about 1 tablespoon of filling in the center of the skin, then fold the skin so the edges touch. Now use the index fingers and thumbs of both hands to fold the skin and pinch it together to create 5 or 6 pleats, pressing each pleat firmly against the flat back layer to seal. The pleats should all face the same direction, creating a gentle curve in the dumpling. Place the finished gyoza on a sheet pan, pleated-side up, and cover with a kitchen towel while you make the rest.

To cook the gyoza, bring a large pot of water to a rolling boil. Gently add the gyoza one at a time, stirring carefully with chopsticks to prevent them from sticking together. Once the water returns to a boil, reduce to a simmer. Cook for about 5 minutes, or until the gyoza float to the surface and the skin appears slightly translucent. The filling should feel firm when gently pressed with chopsticks.

Remove the gyoza with a slotted spoon and serve immediately. Serve with the dipping sauce on the side. Or use the white pepper–vinegar dipping sauce for Lamb Gyoza (page 245) if you prefer. Or use both, which is what we like to do!

P.S. Like with the lamb gyoza, these uncooked gyoza freeze beautifully. Follow the steps on page 246.

HOW TO FORM GYOZA

HOMEMADE GYOZA SKINS

自家製餃子皮

This alternative to store-bought gyoza wrappers is inspired by a grandma we know outside Tokyo who rolls out these babies whenever she's making gyoza (and her gyoza rocks). They're a little thicker than store-bought but the delicate, chewy texture is a delight. The skins are straightforward to make, but you may have to adjust the amount of water to get the right dough consistency. With a little practice you'll get the technique down. We call for half cake flour, half all-purpose flour because the cake variety has less gluten and a softer texture, lending just the right amount of stretchiness for this application.

MAKES ABOUT 24 WRAPPERS

½ cup cake flour, plus more for dusting and rolling

½ cup all-purpose flour

½ teaspoon salt

½ cup hot water

In a medium bowl, whisk together the cake flour, all-purpose flour, and salt until well combined. Pour in the hot water and mix with a wooden spoon until the ingredients start to come together.

Turn the dough out onto a lightly floured work surface and knead with your hands for about 5 minutes until it becomes smooth and firm. The dough should feel soft and bouncy with no stickiness. If it sticks to your fingers, add flour one tablespoon at a time, kneading after each addition. If it feels dry or crumbly, wet your hands lightly and continue kneading.

Form the dough into a ball and cover with a clean kitchen towel. Let it rest at room temperature for 30 minutes. During this time, the dough will become noticeably more pliable—when you press it, it should slowly spring back.

After resting, divide the dough into three equal portions. Roll each portion into a long cylinder, about 12 inches in length. Cut each cylinder into 8 equal pieces, giving you 24 pieces total. Cup each piece in your palm and roll into a smooth ball, then cover with a kitchen towel to prevent drying.

Dust your work surface with flour. Working with one piece at a time, press the dough ball into a flat disk with your palm. Using a rolling pin, roll from the center outward, rotating the wrapper about 30 degrees after each roll, until you have a thin, round wrapper about 3 inches in diameter. If the wrapper starts to stick, dust with more flour.

Stack the finished wrappers with a light dusting of flour between each one to prevent sticking. Keep them covered with a damp towel while you work—the edges should never feel dry or brittle. Use immediately.

SHIBIRE TORI

痺れ鶏

Shibire tori literally means "tingling chicken." We first tasted this dish at one of the Tokyo restaurants of our pal Yoshitoru Ikegawa, Japan's top yakitori chef, who earned a Michelin star for his chicken skewers. He's basically all chicken, all the time (see our Tori Pota Ramen, also inspired by Chef Ikegawa, page 92). When we tasted this dish, which marries moist, juicy breast with a vibrant, fiery sauce laced with tobanjan, fermented soy beans, chile peppers, and sansho, the citrusy Japanese version of Sichuan peppercorns that dance on your tongue (hence, tingling), we immediately grasped our mission: Share a home-cooking version of it with you! So here you go. The super-juicy, just-cooked steamed chicken breast in this recipe is a revelation, so good that we use it twice in this book (also for the Tori Pota Ramen). But why stop there? This chicken is also super delicious served simply with ponzu (see page 129) and a dab of red yuzu kosho (add grated daikon if you have it—it adds flavor and body that helps the ponzu adhere to the meat).

SERVES 4

STEAMED CHICKEN

2 (6-ounce) boneless, skinless chicken breasts

½ teaspoon salt

1 teaspoon sliced ginger

2 tablespoons sake

TINGLING SAUCE

1 teaspoon chopped garlic

1 tablespoon soy sauce

2 teaspoons rice vinegar

1 tablespoon sesame oil

1 tablespoon tobanjan

2 teaspoons honey

1 teaspoon aka miso

GARNISH

½ cup chopped Persian or English cucumber, cut into matchsticks (if you're using English cucumber, peel and remove the seeds)

2 tablespoons peanuts, chopped

¼ cup thinly sliced scallions, white part only

Sansho powder

Prepare the chicken. In a small saucepan that can fit the chicken breasts snugly, add the chicken, salt, ginger, and sake. (The aromatics will infuse the chicken with flavor as it cooks.) Bring to a boil over high heat, then cover, reduce the heat to low, and simmer for 3 minutes. Flip the chicken, cover, and simmer for 3 more minutes. Turn off the heat and let sit covered for 15 minutes. The residual heat will gently cook the chicken through, resulting in super tender, super juicy meat (it'll be just-cooked and ready to eat!). Transfer the chicken to a cutting board, slice it against the grain, cover it loosely, and set aside. Reserve 1 tablespoon of the steaming liquid for the sauce.

Make the tingling sauce. In a small bowl, whisk together the garlic, soy sauce, rice vinegar, sesame oil, tobanjan, honey, and aka miso until well combined. When the chicken is ready, mix in the reserved steaming liquid.

To serve, create a bed of cucumbers on each of four small plates. Arrange the sliced chicken on top of the cucumbers and pour a generous amount of tingling sauce over the chicken, so it drips down onto the cucumber. Sprinkle the chopped peanuts and scallions over each plate and dust with a generous pinch of sansho powder. Serve immediately and mix everything together to eat.

SOY SAUCE ROAST WHOLE CHICKEN

丸鶏醤油焼き

This roasted bird is a tour de force. Full stop. Is it a traditional Japanese dish? No. Is it a modern incarnation of Japanese cuisine? Hell yeah. Here's what makes it so good: First, brining, which makes the meat incredibly moist. And second, *this* brine, which infuses the chicken with the aromatics and astonishing umami-rich Japanese flavors. The slow roast gives the bird the chance to bask in all this goodness, while basting it with toasted sesame oil lavishes another flavor layer and burnishes the skin a rich bronze. Enjoy this chicken as an element of a Japanese meal (or any meal). Or let it come to room temperature and layer boneless pieces atop Kimchi Ramen (page 87) or some other noodle dish. (We stumbled on this phenomenal combo when cooking the chicken and kimchi ramen on the same day in our test kitchen, a.k.a. Harris's apartment, and haven't looked back.) This chicken tastes amazing cold, too; there's really no bad way to eat it. One last note: Do not discard the carcass. If you do, we'll have a major bone to pick with you. Seriously, don't throw out the bones! Use them to make an incredible stock. Think about it—a broth teased from bones infused with Japanese flavors and amped up with more aromatics! Use the stock for noodles, soups, and more. We share the method after the recipe.

SERVES 4 TO 6

BRINE

4 cups water

1 cup soy sauce

¼ cup sake

2 tablespoons sugar

2-inch piece ginger, unpeeled and sliced

3 to 4 garlic cloves, peeled and crushed

½ bunch scallions, trimmed and roughly chopped

1 (3- to 4-pound) whole chicken

1 tablespoon toasted sesame oil

In a large bowl or container, combine all the brine ingredients and mix well until the sugar dissolves. Submerge the chicken in the brine, ensuring it's completely covered. If needed, place a plate on top to keep the chicken submerged. Refrigerate for 24 hours.

(If your bowl isn't large enough for the chicken to be fully submerged, start breast-side down and flip halfway through.)

Remove the chicken from the brine. Pat the chicken dry thoroughly with paper towels and let it sit at room temperature for about 1 hour before roasting. Meanwhile, preheat your oven to 400°F.

Place the chicken, breast-side up, in a large cast-iron skillet (ideal because the iron captures heat for superior caramelization) or a large roasting pan. Brush the entire surface

CONTINUED →

SOY SAUCE ROAST WHOLE CHICKEN, CONTINUED

of the chicken with half of the sesame oil. This will help the skin crisp up and add a wonderful aroma. Roast the chicken for 30 minutes, then brush the remaining sesame oil over it to keep the chicken moist and add flavor. Roast for 30 minutes more.

Keep an eye on the chicken while it's roasting. Check for doneness at the 1 hour mark by making a cut between the leg and thigh. If the juices run clear, the bird is ready. If not, roast for an additional 10 to 15 minutes and check again. But be careful not to overcook and dry out the chicken (you brined it for a reason).

When you pull the chicken out of the oven, the skin should be a nice bronze and you should smell an incredible, incredible savory aroma. (Did we say incredible?) Let the chicken rest for 5 to 10 minutes before carving. This allows the juices to redistribute throughout the meat. To serve, carve the chicken and arrange the pieces on a platter. Pour the remaining pan juices over for extra flavor.

CHICKEN STOCK

Place the chicken carcass in a medium pot. (A 3-quart pot or Dutch oven works well for a single chicken carcass.) Break it up a bit if needed to fit comfortably. Add a couple of scallions (green and white parts), a few crushed garlic cloves (no need to peel), and a thumb-size piece of ginger, also unpeeled, sliced. Fill the pot with enough cold water to cover. Bring the water to a boil over medium-high heat, then reduce the heat to low and let it simmer gently for about 2 hours. Skim off any scum that rises to the surface during the cooking. Let the stock cool before straining through a fine-mesh sieve (discard the solids). You can freeze the stock for up to 6 months.

WEEKNIGHT CHICKEN . . . IN A HURRY!

Gotta feed yourself, a significant other, and/or hangry kids after a busy day breaking rocks (metaphorically or otherwise)? As per usual, we got you! Here are three delicious, super-fast methods to add to your weeknight playbook: Season boneless chicken breast or thigh with salt and pan-sauté or broil, and serve with a dollop of green yuzu kosho; season boneless breast or thigh with salt and pan-sauté or broil, and serve with ponzu and daikon oroshi (as with our roasted veggies, see page 129); or season boneless breast or thigh with salt and sansho and pan-sauté or broil, and serve with a wedge of lemon (a favorite staff meal at Tadashi's restaurants). You're welcome!

CHiKUZEN-Ni

(CHICKEN BRAISED WITH ROOT VEGETABLES)

筑前煮

Chikuzen-ni is one of the first dishes that Harris mastered when he taught himself how to cook Japanese. And he had the guts back then (or was it foolishness?) to serve his version to a Japanese government official. But, hey, she liked it! In this hearty *nimono,* or simmered dish, chicken and root vegetables are cooked together with Japanese seasonings and shiitake, a fortuitous marriage that yields deep savory, chicken-y, and earthy flavors and looks just lovely with all those vibrant vegetables. And it's easy for anyone, including a duffer like early-Japanese-cooking-Harris, to knock this nimono out of the park. Chikuzen-ni is a go-to dish in, spitballing here, no less than 99 percent of Japanese homes (and we stand by that number!). Besides being extremely delicious hot or cold—it gets better the next day—this dish offers a master class in utilizing two key Japanese cooking techniques: the rangiri cut and the one and only otoshibuta, or drop lid (see pages 209 and 210 for a deep dive on both).

SERVES 4

6 ounces burdock root

1 (10-ounce) lotus root, peeled and sliced into ½-inch half-moons

2 medium carrots (about 6 ounces total), cut rangiri style (we don't peel)

5 dried shiitake mushrooms, soaked in 1½ cups water for about 1 hour

1 tablespoon sesame oil

1 pound chicken thighs, boned and cut into about 2-inch cubes (with the skin on preferably)

¼ cup soy sauce

¼ cup sake

¼ cup mirin

2 tablespoons finely sliced scallions, greens only

Begin by preparing the vegetables. Under cold running water, use steel wool or a scrubby to gently rub off the brown exterior of the burdock root until you see the pale white flesh (it doesn't have to be perfect). Cut it rangiri style and soak it in a bowl filled with cold water to prevent discoloration. Set aside. In a separate bowl, soak the sliced lotus root in water to remove starch and prevent discoloration. No soaking for the carrots.

Squeeze the excess water from the soaked shiitake mushrooms, reserving 1 cup of the soaking liquid. Trim the stems from the mushrooms and cut the caps in half. Set aside.

Heat the sesame oil in a large pot over medium heat. Add the chicken pieces and cook, stirring constantly, for about 2 minutes, or until the exterior turns white. You're not trying to cook the chicken through at this point, just sealing in the juices.

Drain the burdock root and add it to the pot. Cook, stirring frequently, for 1 minute. Then drain and add the lotus root and cook for another minute. Add the carrots, stir, and cook for 1 more minute. You want all the vegetables to be nicely coated with the sesame oil. Stir gently and be careful not to break

CONTINUED →

apart the vegetables. Finally, add the shiitake mushrooms and stir to combine. Pour in the reserved shiitake soaking liquid and the soy sauce, sake, and mirin. Bring the liquid to a boil, then reduce the heat to low. Make sure to skim off any scum that appears on the surface, which can affect the flavor.

Now it's otoshibuta time! Place the drop lid directly on top of the ingredients in the pot. Reduce the heat to medium-low or low so you achieve a gentle simmer (adjust as necessary for your stove). You'll see the otoshibuta resting on the ingredients, with steam escaping (if the otoshibuta is bouncing around, lower the heat). Cook this way undisturbed for 30 minutes. Just leave the dang thing alone and give the otoshibuta time to work its magic.

Remove the pot from the heat and let it cool for about 10 minutes. The flavors will continue to develop as it cools. (Many Japanese cooks believe chikuzen-ni tastes even better the next day, after the ingredients have had time to fully absorb the savory-sweet cooking liquid.)

Remove the otoshibuta, garnish with the scallions, and serve.

P.S. If you can't find burdock root and/or lotus root, don't sweat it. Substitute with more carrots or parsnips or even celery root. These substitutions will change the character of the dish, but isn't that half the fun? If you try this, let us know how it came out.

RANGIRI CUTTING TECHNIQUE

Rangiri literally means "random cut." It's anything but. This ingenious method for cutting irregular-size root vegetables creates pieces that are roughly uniform, so they cook evenly. It also creates more surface area on each piece, allowing it to cook faster and absorb flavors better. And it helps vegetables maintain their shape during long cooking processes like nimono. And—yeah, the fun never stops—the irregular shapes also make dishes more visually interesting. To cut carrots, burdock, daikon, cucumbers, sweet potatoes, and other vegetables rangiri style, first angle your knife 30 to 40 degrees to the root. Slice and then rotate the vegetable a quarter turn (90 degrees) along its axis. Repeat this angled cutting and rotating until you work your way through the whole thing. Practice this technique a few times and you'll master it, promise. (And use it for all your cooking, not only Japanese, for all manner of stews and soups—they'll taste better.)

THE (AMAZING) OTOSHIBUTA

This is a genius piece of Japanese kitchen equipment. The *otoshibuta,* or drop lid, is a covering smaller than the diameter of a saucepan or pot, so it fits inside directly on top of the cooking ingredients instead of just covering them (hence, “drop lid”). So what’s the big whoop about that? Well, four whoops to be exact: First, the otoshibuta circulates and increases heat, so ingredients cook quicker and more evenly. Second, the higher temperature it creates caramelizes sugars in the cooking liquid, which adds mouthwatering flavor and evaporates and concentrates the cooking liquid. Third, it causes the cooking liquid to circulate in the saucepan, coating the ingredients without having to stir them. And finally, the otoshibuta holds ingredients in place so they don’t move around and break apart while cooking. We said *genius* for a reason! In Japan you can buy wooden or plastic otoshibuta in various sizes (available here online, but stick with the wooden ones), but we rely on an easy workaround—good ol’ aluminum foil. Just fold a double-layered piece of aluminum foil into a circle smaller than the diameter of your pot. Then simply drop it over your bubbling ingredients! It should not be so perfect that it completely seals in the cooking liquid; you want steam to be able to escape.

NEXT-LEVEL KARAAGE

究極の鶏唐揚げ

Here's the thing. There's no better fried chicken than Japanese-style fried chicken, called *karaage* ("karra-agh-eh"). Why? Chunks of flavorful dark meat chicken are first marinated in savory seasonings before being dredged in potato starch and deep-fried. So flavor is locked into every crispy, juicy, heavenly bite. It doesn't get better than that. Wait, actually it does. In this version, Tadashi builds on perfection: First, he brines the chicken so it stays even more juicy while frying. Second, he mixes rice flour into the potato starch, which delivers even more crispness. And third, he adds water to the mixture, so when the wet coating hits the hot oil, it creates an incredibly lacy, tempura-ish crust. Oh, and we use extra-large chunks of dark meat in this recipe—to give you more chew time to enjoy this fantastic fried chicken! Brining and marinating in this recipe take about 1 hour, so factor that into your cook time.

SERVES 4

1 pound chicken thigh meat, cut into 2- to 3-inch pieces

1 lemon, cut into wedges

BRINE

2 teaspoons salt

2 cups water

MARINADE

2 tablespoons sake

2 tablespoons soy sauce

1 teaspoon salt

2 tablespoons freshly grated ginger

2 teaspoons sesame oil

1 teaspoon ground white pepper

YUZU MAYO

½ cup mayonnaise

1 tablespoon yuzu juice (or 2 teaspoons lemon juice)

1 teaspoon green yuzu kosho

COATING

1 cup potato starch (katakuriko)

½ cup rice flour

¼ cup water

Cooking oil for frying

Brine the chicken. In a large bowl, combine the salt and water and stir to dissolve the salt. Add the chicken pieces and let them brine, uncovered, for 30 minutes at room temperature.

Meanwhile, prepare the marinade. In a medium bowl, combine the sake, soy sauce, salt, grated ginger, sesame oil, and white pepper.

Remove the chicken from the brine and pat the pieces thoroughly dry with paper towels, to get rid of excess water that would dilute the marinade. Add the chicken to the marinade, mixing well to ensure each piece is coated. Cover and let marinate for 30 minutes at room temperature.

Prepare the yuzu mayo. In a small bowl, whisk together the mayo, yuzu juice, and yuzu kosho. Set aside.

Make the coating. In a large bowl, whisk together the potato starch and rice flour. Slowly add the water, combining it with your hands until the mixture resembles coarse cornmeal.

Prepare a deep-fry station. (Important: Read our note on deep-frying first, see page 213.) Fill a large cast-iron skillet or heavy-bottomed pot with at least 1½ inches of oil, enough so the chicken will float when it cooks. Attach a deep-fry or

CONTINUED →

candy thermometer to the side of the skillet and heat the oil to 350°F over medium heat. It's crucial to use a thermometer to maintain the correct temperature throughout the frying process. On a work surface near the burner, prepare a paper towel–lined plate to drain the cooked chicken.

When the chicken is ready, squeeze off any excess marinade with your hands and dredge the chicken in the potato starch mixture. Place the dredged pieces on a plate and repeat until all the chicken is coated.

When the oil temperature reaches 350°F, carefully add the chicken to the hot oil, working in batches to avoid overcrowding. (Use at most half of the surface area of the oil to cook.) Adjust the heat throughout the cooking time to maintain the oil temperature at about 350°F. Cook the chicken for about 5 minutes, turning once at the 3-minute mark. The chicken will be golden brown, incredibly crispy, and super juicy inside thanks to the brining. Transfer the fried chicken to the prepared plate.

Serve the karaage immediately or at room temperature, with lemon wedges and the yuzu mayo for dipping. (Karaage is a perfect picnic food.)

A WORD, OR THREE, ABOUT DEEP-FRYING

Deep-frying is a contact sport. What we mean is, you have to be present. Sliding a roast into the oven and clicking on a timer this ain't. When the chicken, or other ingredient, hits the hot oil, the temperature will drop. That's okay. Keep watching and adjusting the heat throughout the cooking time to maintain the target temperature. (A deep-fry or candy thermometer is crucial to this process; make sure to use one.) And if it's a little higher, don't sweat it—just lower the heat to get to the right temp. But deep-frying is not only about thermometer vigilance. Keep an eye on the frying ingredients themselves. You're aiming for golden brown. Deep-frying moves fast. Are the ingredients getting *too* browned or starting to burn? Lower the heat or pull them out of the oil, for goodness' sake! The recipes we share are solid guidelines. But ingredients vary, of course, by weight, or even how cold they are coming out of the fridge. If you remember anything, remember this: *Use your judgment.* With a little practice, you'll be deep-frying like a pro.

"BUFFALO" MISO TEBASAKI

(CHICKEN WINGS)

味噌バッファロー手羽先

When it comes to chicken, Nagoya doesn't mess around. A ninety-minute bullet train shot from Tokyo, this city is a chicken lover's dream, and even boasts its own bespoke breed, called Nagoya Cochin, served grilled, deep-fried, steamed, or as *torisashi*—raw chicken sashimi (so incredibly good but a bridge too far for this book!). Chicken wings (*tebasaki*) hold pride of place. Tossed in a sweet sauce, slathered in a peppery soy sauce, or glazed in a sweet-savory miso sauce, wings inspire passionate followings among locals; so much so, there's even an annual "chicken wing war" between two iconic wing joints. But we're not taking sides. Instead, we offer this delicious take on Nagoya miso wings, with a nod to another wing-crazed city's eponymous version. Make sure to eat these with a frosty beer at the ready (preferably a Sapporo or Kirin).

SERVES 4

2 pounds chicken wings

4 cups cold water

2 teaspoons salt

1 tablespoon sugar

Vegetable oil for deep-frying

½ cup potato starch (katakuriko)

SAUCE

½ cup aka miso

3 tablespoons sugar

3 tablespoons sake

2 tablespoons mirin

¼ cup Worcestershire sauce

1 tablespoon ketchup

¼ small onion, chopped

1 celery rib, chopped

1 tablespoon chopped garlic

1 tablespoon chopped ginger

2 teaspoons tobanjan

1 teaspoon Tabasco sauce

1 teaspoon togarashi

½ cup chicken stock (preferably low-sodium, or use homemade, see page 206)

FOR GARNISH

1 teaspoon toasted black sesame seeds

2 tablespoons finely sliced scallions

Brine the wings. Cut off the wing tips and discard. Separate the flat part from the drumette at the joint, creating two pieces from each wing. Trim off any excess fat. In a large bowl, stir together the water, salt, and sugar. Add the chicken wings and let them brine, uncovered, for 1 hour at room temperature. This will make them plump and juicy.

In a large saucepan, combine the sauce ingredients. Bring to a boil over medium heat, then reduce the heat and simmer, stirring occasionally, for about 5 minutes. Remove from the heat and let cool slightly. Transfer to a blender and blend until smooth, about 2 minutes. Pour the sauce into a large bowl and set aside.

Prepare a deep-fry station. (Important: Read our note on deep-frying first, see page 213.) Fill a large cast-iron skillet or heavy-bottomed pot with at least 2 inches of oil, enough so the wings will float when they cook. Attach a deep-fry or candy thermometer to the side of the skillet and heat the oil to 350°F over medium heat. It's crucial to use a thermometer to maintain the correct temperature throughout the frying process. On a work surface near the burner, prepare a paper towel–lined plate to drain the cooked wings.

Drain the wings and pat them dry with paper towels to remove excess moisture. Place the potato starch in a shallow medium bowl. Lightly dredge the wings in the potato starch, shaking off any excess.

Carefully add the wings to the hot oil, working in batches to avoid overcrowding. (Use at most half of the surface area of the oil to cook.) Adjust the heat throughout the cooking time to maintain the temperature at about 350°F. Cook the wings for about 10 minutes, turning them occasionally so they cook evenly and don't stick to the bottom of the pot, until golden brown and they float to the top of the oil. The flat parts may cook faster than the drumettes so you may need to remove them earlier. Transfer to the prepared plate to drain.

Add the fried wings to the bowl with the sauce and toss with a large spoon or kitchen chopsticks (saibashi) to make sure each piece is thoroughly coated. Transfer the coated wings to a large serving platter and sprinkle them with the black sesame seeds and scallions. Go to town.

TORi NANBAN SANDO

鶏南蛮サンド

Words can flip meanings as the centuries roll by (case in point, *clue* once meant "balls of yarn"—huh?). In Japanese, *nanban* literally translates to "southern barbarian." In the sixteenth century it referred to Portuguese traders who arrived in Japan at the time. But jump ahead four hundred years, and the meaning has turned on its head: It now denotes something foreign and highly desirable in Japanese cuisine, and honors a cooking style inspired by Portuguese influences that involves deep-frying and serving with, or marinating in, a tangy sauce. And that's what we get with this fantastic sandwich, where chicken is dredged in flour and dipped in egg before frying—no breading needed. The result is a thin, crispy crust that locks in the chicken's natural juices. Tori nanban is typically served with a Japanese-style tartar sauce, and while in Japan this sandwich employs slices of toasted milk bread, try it with a brioche roll, pretzel roll, hero roll, or even baguette.

SERVES 4

TARTAR SAUCE

½ cup mayonnaise

¼ cup finely chopped pickles or cornichons

2 hard-boiled eggs, chopped

2 tablespoons finely chopped red onion

1 tablespoon ketchup

2 teaspoons lemon juice

2 teaspoons chopped shiso (or parsley)

1 teaspoon wasabi

4 (4-ounce) boneless, skin-on chicken thighs

Salt and ground white pepper

¼ cup all-purpose flour

2 eggs, beaten

Vegetable oil for frying

8 slices Japanese milk bread (or good-quality white bread)

4 iceberg or romaine lettuce leaves

Make the tartar sauce. In a small bowl, whisk together the mayo, pickles, eggs, onion, ketchup, lemon juice, shiso, and wasabi. Set aside.

Lay the chicken thighs flat on a cutting board, skin-side down. Using a knife, make small cuts in the flesh to help it cook evenly. Season generously with salt and white pepper on both sides.

Set up a dredging station: Place the flour on one plate, beaten eggs on another, and leave a third plate empty for the dredged chicken. Dredge each chicken thigh in flour, shaking off excess. Then dip in the egg, allowing excess to drip off. Place on the empty plate.

Prepare a deep-fry station. (Important: Read our note on deep-frying first, see page 213.) Fill a large cast-iron skillet or heavy-bottomed pot with at least 2 inches of oil, enough so the chicken will float when it cooks. Attach a deep-fry or candy thermometer to the side of the skillet and heat the oil to 350°F over medium heat. It's crucial to use a thermometer to maintain the correct temperature throughout the frying process. On a work surface near the burner, prepare a paper towel–lined plate to drain the cooked chicken.

CONTINUED →

TORi NANBAN SANDO, CONTINUED

Carefully add the chicken to the hot oil, working in batches to avoid overcrowding (use at most half of the surface area of the oil to cook). Adjust the heat throughout the cooking time to maintain the temperature at about 350°F. Cook the chicken for about 10 minutes, turning once, until golden brown and cooked through. Transfer the chicken to the prepared plate to drain.

While the chicken is cooking, toast the bread.

To assemble the sandwiches, place a lettuce leaf on a slice of toast, then lay a piece of fried chicken on top. Slather the chicken with a generous helping of tartar sauce. Top with another slice of toast and cut in half diagonally. Repeat with the remaining ingredients and serve the sandwiches immediately, while the chicken is still hot and crispy.

NANBAN SAUCE OPTION

If you're not feeling a sandwich, try the chicken sans bread with a classic nanban sauce. To make the sauce, in a small saucepan, combine 2 tablespoons rice vinegar, 2 tablespoons soy sauce, 2 tablespoons mirin, and 1 teaspoon sugar. Stir to dissolve the sugar and bring the liquid to a boil over medium-high heat. As soon as it boils, turn off the heat. When the chicken is ready, dip it into the nanban sauce, flipping the cooked chicken so both sides are generously coated. Pull the chicken out, slice, spoon some tartar sauce over, and go to town! (Or, just as fantastic, enjoy with the nanban sauce and a squeeze of lemon.)

DUCK WONTONS

鴨ワンタン

Gyoza isn't the only dumpling game in (a Japanese) town. Consider the wonton. These amazing Chinese dumplings landed in Japan sometime after World War II and quickly became a beloved dish. Interestingly, gyoza also claims Chinese roots (progeny of *jiaozi*) and quickly gained all-star Japanese food status. Wontons, on the other hand, are still considered Chinese food in Japan but have been adapted to local tastes. Wherever they come from, we love all versions of wontons! The recipe here is a favorite of Tadashi's, centering on duck dumplings smothered in a beautiful chicken-y, gingery sauce.

SERVES 4 (MAKES ABOUT 16 WONTONS)

1 (½-pound) boneless duck breast

¼ cup finely chopped scallions, white part only

1 tablespoon finely chopped ginger

1 teaspoon finely chopped garlic

¼ teaspoon black pepper

¼ teaspoon sansho pepper

1 teaspoon soy sauce

1 teaspoon mirin

1 teaspoon orange zest

1 teaspoon potato starch (katakuriko)

3 tablespoons warm water

16 wonton skins

SAUCE

2 cups chicken stock (preferably low-sodium, or use homemade, see page 206)

2 tablespoons soy sauce

1 tablespoon mirin

1 tablespoon thinly sliced ginger

¼ cup thinly sliced scallions, green part (mottai-nai, see page 49)

Prepare the duck meat. Trim excess fat from the duck, but don't go overboard; some fat to adds rich flavor to these wontons. In a food processor, pulse the duck meat for about 30 seconds until it's finely minced. Be careful not to overprocess; you want it finely chopped, not turned into a paste.

In a large bowl, combine the duck meat, scallions, ginger, garlic, black pepper, sansho pepper, soy sauce, mirin, and orange zest. Using your hands, mix vigorously for about 60 seconds until the mixture becomes slightly sticky. This kneading action will help bind the ingredients together and create a springier texture in the cooked wontons.

In a small bowl, whisk the potato starch and the warm water. This is the "glue" for sealing the wontons.

Place a wonton skin flour-side up in the palm of your hand. Dip your finger in the potato starch mixture and wet the edges of the skin. Place about two teaspoons of the duck mixture in the center of the skin. Fold the wrapper over to form a triangle, pressing the edges to seal. Repeat until you've used all the filling. Place the finished wontons on a plate in single layer so they don't stick together. Set aside.

CONTINUED →

DUCK WONTONS, CONTINUED

Bring a large pot of unsalted water to a boil.

While the water is heating, make the sauce. Combine the chicken stock, soy sauce, mirin, and ginger in a saucepan and bring to a boil over medium heat. Reduce the heat to low and simmer the sauce for about 5 minutes to let the flavors meld. Keep warm over very low heat while you cook the wontons.

Gently add the wontons to the boiling water, stirring carefully to prevent sticking (saibashi, or kitchen chopsticks, are ideal for this task). Cook for 2 to 3 minutes, or until they float to the surface and the wrappers become translucent.

Remove the cooked wontons with a slotted spoon and divide them among four bowls. Ladle the sauce over the wontons. Garnish with the sliced scallions and serve immediately.

P.S. If you're pinched for time, you can make an old-fashioned dipping sauce instead of the sauce here. Just mix together 3 tablespoons soy sauce, 3 tablespoons rice vinegar, and 1 tablespoon rayu chili oil (see page 245). Divide into four small shallow bowls and dip away. (Perfect for gyoza, too.)

KAMO JiBUNi

鴨治部煮

If you're ever trying to figure out what to serve a samurai for dinner, we got you! This duck dish stretches back something like four hundred years and was notable in the old days as a celebration food enjoyed by both regular folk and *katana*-toting warriors alike. But hey, you don't need a special occasion—or a sword—to whip up kamo jibuni! In this dish, traditionally served in the winter, we lightly poach duck slices along with mushrooms and carrot in a savory dashi-powered broth. The key here is dredging the duck in potato starch (a super old Japanese cooking technique originally done with arrowroot starch), which not only seals in the meat's juicy flavor but also adds a beautiful silky texture to the duck-infused broth. This dish also works nicely with sliced chicken breast, sliced red snapper, or halibut.

SERVES 4

2 skinless duck breasts (about 1 pound)

Salt

1 small bunch spinach (about 4 ounces), trimmed

2 cups dashi (see page 40)

¼ cup mirin

2 tablespoons soy sauce

1 medium carrot (about 1 ounce), sliced into ¼-inch-thick rounds

1 cup stemmed and sliced shiitake mushrooms (about 2 ounces)

1 cup shimeji mushrooms (about 2 ounces), separated into small clusters

1 to 2 tablespoons potato starch (katakuriko) (just enough for dredging)

2 teaspoons wasabi

Trim any excess fat from the duck breasts and cut into ¼ inch slices. Lightly salt the slices on both sides to tenderize. Let them rest, uncovered, at room temperature for 15 minutes.

Fill a medium bowl with cold water. Place a large pot of water over high heat. As soon as the water boils add the spinach and blanch for 30 seconds. Immediately transfer the spinach to the cold water to stop the cooking. When the spinach cools, drain and set aside.

In a medium saucepan over medium heat, combine the dashi, mirin, and soy sauce. When the liquid begins to simmer, add the carrot, shiitake, and shimeji mushrooms. Simmer gently for about 5 minutes, or until the carrot is tender. Reduce the heat to low.

While the carrots and mushrooms are simmering, coat the duck slices with the potato starch, shaking off any excess.

Gently add the duck slices to the simmering broth, keeping them separate (so they're not all clumped together). Poach for about 5 minutes, or until the duck is cooked through but still tender.

To serve, divide the duck and vegetables among four bowls, then ladle the hot broth over them. Top each bowl with a portion of the blanched spinach and a dollop of wasabi. Encourage diners to mix the wasabi into the broth before diving in.

9

BEEF, PORK, AND LAMB

牛、豚、羊

In the late nineteenth century, when Japan emerged from three hundred years of self-isolation, Emperor Meiji encountered strapping American and European soldiers and sailors nourished on the health food of the day—mountains of meat. He promptly reversed a thousand-year ban on meat eating in the country. But while Japanese people embraced meat, they did so on their own terms. To this day, thinly sliced, tender cuts of beef—rather than dense slabs of dry-aged T-bone—are preferred, a nod to chopstick culture and a more natural fit for a cuisine where delicate fish is fundamental. The apex of Japanese beef is incredibly rich and flavorful *wagyu,* a style of meat that expresses the nexus of topography, cuisine, and culture (see page 231). Pork and lamb have their own stories to tell of how they landed in Japanese cooking, which we'll talk about later (naturally!). Like with chicken, these meats resonate with Japanese fermented and umami flavors, a sensibility you'll appreciate as you cook the dishes in this chapter.

JAPANESE BEER

Ah, Japanese beer. Crisp, refreshing, light, and clean. It pairs perfectly with the cuisine. Roll into any *izakaya* (eating pub) in Japan and you'll hear shouts of "nama biru onegaishimasu" (draft beer, please!) and "toriaezu biru" (basically, bring the damn beer!), the traditional first round of drinks to break the ice, lubricate the palate, and get a meal going.

Dutch traders introduced beer to Japan four hundred years ago, but it wasn't until the late nineteenth century that it caught fire as a popular drink (the first commercial brewery, what is today's Kirin, was started by an American in 1869). Japanese beers were originally modeled after German lagers, but as with many aspects of Japanese culture, this foreign import evolved into its own distinctive thing, a brewing tradition defined by a lighter body, crisper taste, and drier finish than European beers. Many producers also add rice to their recipes, which result in a lower malt content and a more delicate flavor. These brews complement rather than overwhelm Japanese meals. In fact, the light carbonation and subtle sweetness of Japanese beers actually enhances and intensifies the umami flavors in the cooking.

We love these classic Japanese beers:

- Asahi Super Dry
- Kirin Ichiban Shibori
- Suntory The Premium Malt's (not a typo)
- Sapporo Black Label

Finally, we want to note that, starting in the mid-1990s, laws changed to allow craft beer production, resulting in an explosion of ja-biru, or "local beer," as microbreweries are known. If you're into craft beer, these brewers are producing a wide range of beautiful flavors and styles. Check out beers by Hitachino, Yona Yona, Echigo, and others.

NiKU TOFU
(BRAISED BEEF AND TOFU)
肉豆腐

We originally set out to share a recipe for niku jaga, a homey favorite centered on beef and potatoes braised in Japanese seasonings, inspired, so the story goes, by the beef stews cooked aboard British naval vessels calling on Japanese ports in the early twentieth century. But then we grabbed a bite at Nanca, a tiny, cool spot in the hip Yoyogi Uehara neighborhood of Tokyo, where Chihiro Hagiwara, the talented chef there, reinterpreted this dish just by swapping out the potatoes for tofu. Wow! We loved it, and also loved the fact that her niku tofu expresses modern Japanese cooking not by incorporating unfamiliar ingredients, but by remixing age-old ones. The result is a deeply flavorful and satisfying dish that's lighter than the traditional version and amplified by the sublime taste and texture of tofu. So of course we had to pass it on to you! The squiggly shirataki noodles in this recipe, made from the konjac yam, become soft and tender but don't taste like much. In a dish like this their job is to absorb all the flavors swirling about and add wonderful texture, which they do admirably. (They're also fun to eat.) Finally, we use the thin-sliced beef that you find in Japanese or Korean markets, but if that's not available, substitute with ground beef.

SERVES 4

1 (14-ounce) package firm tofu

1 (7-ounce) package shirataki noodles

1 medium onion

2 cups water

¼ cup soy sauce

¼ cup mirin

¼ cup sake

1 tablespoon sugar

1 tablespoon vegetable oil

1 pound thin-sliced beef, cut into roughly 1-inch squares (or ground beef)

1 tablespoon chopped scallions, green part only, cut on the diagonal ½ inch thick

Drain the tofu. To remove as much water as possible, place the tofu on a plate in the sink and rest another plate or small skillet on top of it. Let sit for about 5 minutes. This pushes water out and will allow the tofu to sponge up the braising liquid. Cut the pressed tofu into 8 pieces. Or go bigger and badder and cut the tofu into 4 huge pieces, for dramatic effect! Set aside.

Next, rinse the shirataki noodles thoroughly under cold water to remove any packaging liquid. Cut the onion in half, tip to tail, then cut into ½-inch-thick slices. Form an aluminum foil otoshibuta (drop lid, see page 210). Set everything aside.

In a medium bowl, combine the water, soy sauce, mirin, sake, and sugar and stir until the sugar dissolves. Set aside.

In a heavy-bottomed pot (an enameled cast-iron pot or Dutch oven is ideal) heat the oil over medium heat. Add the onion and cook, stirring constantly, for about 1 minute until it starts to become translucent. Add the beef and cook, stirring frequently to break apart the meat and brown it slightly, about 2 minutes.

Add the shirataki and gently stir to combine. Pour in the soy sauce mixture and increase the heat to high. Gently add the tofu to the pot, being careful not to break up the pieces (but if they crumble a bit, that's okay!). Stir very carefully to combine the tofu with the beef and shirataki.

Remove any scum that appears on the surface. As soon as the liquid boils, reduce the heat to medium-low.

Place the otoshibuta directly on top of the ingredients in the pot. Adjust the heat to a gentle simmer. You should see the otoshibuta resting on top of the ingredients, with steam escaping—if the otoshibuta is bouncing around, lower the heat. Cook undisturbed for 30 minutes, until the cooking liquid is thickened and glossy and the aroma is blowing your mind.

Serve in individual bowls or place the niku tofu in a big bowl for sharing. Garnish with the scallions and serve immediately. Like with other Japanese braised dishes, niku tofu will taste even better the next day, after the flavors have had a chance to meld further.

VARIATION

If you want to go straight-up traditional niku jaga, just swap the tofu for 1½ pounds Yukon Gold potatoes, cut into about 2-inch pieces. Add the potatoes after the beef and cook, gently stirring, for about 2 minutes, which will help prevent them from breaking up during cooking. Now follow the rest of the recipe (without the tofu, of course).

MISO FLAT IRON STEAK
牛三筋味噌焼き

Butchers knew something we didn't. Forget porterhouse, strip, or T-bone. Flat iron was their secret jam. Known as a "butcher's cut," they'd save this humbler and less pricey piece of beef for their family back in the day. Incredibly tender and intensely beefy, it's now widely available (sorry, butchers). This succulent steak, called *misuji,* marries perfectly with Japanese flavors. Here we pair it with hatcho miso (see page 98), whose bold, intense umami flavor and subtle bitterness and tanginess serve as a mouthwatering counterpoint to the tender beef. The hatcho here is reminiscent of the role bittersweet, earthy mole plays in Mexican cuisine. If you love steak, you will love this recipe, which also works great with another classic butcher's cut, hanger steak. Make sure to have all your ingredients prepped before you get going; this is fast cooking.

SERVES 4

1 (1- to 1½-pound) flat iron steak, about ¾ to 1 inch thick, trimmed of excess fat

Salt and freshly ground black pepper

2 tablespoons hatcho miso (or aka miso)

1 tablespoon mirin

¼ cup red wine

1 tablespoon sesame oil

½ cup finely chopped onion

1 teaspoon finely chopped garlic

1 tablespoon sake

1 tablespoon Shibori Scallions (page 41)

2 teaspoons toasted white sesame seeds

Season the steak generously with salt and pepper on both sides. Let it sit, uncovered, at room temperature while you prepare the other ingredients, for at least 10 minutes.

In a small bowl, whisk together the hatcho miso, mirin, and red wine until the hatcho dissolves. Set aside.

Heat the sesame oil in a large skillet (we like to use a cast-iron skillet) over medium heat. Add the steak and cook for 3 minutes, until nicely browned. Flip and cook for 2 more minutes. Add the onion and garlic around the meat (not on top) and cook for about 30 seconds, using cooking chopsticks or tongs to move the steak around so the aromatics cook evenly without burning. The onion and garlic will become fragrant and just start to turn translucent.

Add the sake and cook for about 30 seconds. Add the miso mixture and cook for 1 minute. Flip the steak and cook for another minute, until the sauce has the consistency of ketchup. For medium-rare, the steak should feel like the fleshy part between your thumb and forefinger.

Remove from the heat, cover, and let the steak rest in the pan for 5 minutes. During this time, flip the steak once or twice in the sauce to coat.

Transfer the steak to a cutting board and slice it against the grain into about ¼-inch-thick pieces. ("Slicing against the grain" means slicing perpendicular to the muscle fibers, which are the long strands you can see running in parallel lines through the meat. This technique shortens these tough muscle fibers, making each bite more tender and easier to chew.)

Arrange the slices on a serving plate, spoon the sauce over the meat, and garnish with the shibori scallions and sesame seeds. Serve immediately.

P.S. Leftover steak can be stored in its sauce for up to 2 days in the refrigerator; gently reheat in a covered pan over low heat. (Basically, the world's best leftovers.)

WAGYU SANDO

和牛サンド

Wagyu, which simply means "Japanese cow," is a national treasure. Developed through selective breeding due to limited grazing space, these prized cows are raised in special stress-free environments, chug beer to stimulate their appetites, and are treated to sake massages to improve their amazing meat quality. Nice life. (Okay, at least until you-know-what.) The result of all this effort? Luscious, intensely marbled, melt-in-your-mouth beef. There's no other like it. So rich and beefy and sublime. It's more of a treat than something you want to eat every day, unless you have a crush on your cardiologist. But if you're into beef, wagyu is the meat mountain top. Naturally, all this beefy ecstasy comes at a steep price, but luckily, there's now something called American Wagyu, which is more affordable.

SERVES 4

4 ciabatta rolls (or a crusty baguette cut into 4 portions)

1 pound shredded American wagyu beef

Salt and freshly ground black pepper

1 teaspoon tobanjan

1 tablespoon mirin

1 tablespoon sake

1 tablespoon soy sauce

1 teaspoon sugar

1 tablespoon sesame oil

¼ medium onion, thinly sliced

1 garlic clove, thinly sliced

4 green leaf lettuce leaves (or other tender lettuce)

1 teaspoon black sesame seeds (or white sesame seeds)

Split and toast the rolls. Set aside while you cook the meat; this dish comes together quickly.

Lightly season the wagyu with salt and pepper.

In a small bowl, whisk together the tobanjan, mirin, sake, soy sauce, and sugar.

Heat a large skillet over medium heat. Add the sesame oil, then the onion, and cook, stirring constantly, for about 1 minute, until the onion just starts to become translucent. Add the garlic and cook, stirring constantly so the garlic doesn't burn, for 30 seconds more.

Increase the heat to medium-high and add the seasoned wagyu. Using cooking chopsticks (which are ideal for this) or tongs, keep stirring and separating the pieces of meat. Cook for about 1 minute, until the meat just loses its pink but isn't browned.

Pour in the soy mixture and continue to cook, stirring constantly, for another 1 to 2 minutes, until most of the liquid has evaporated but the meat is still juicy. Don't overcook; the meat should still be tender.

To assemble the sandwiches, lay the lettuce on the bottom halves of the toasted rolls and top with the hot meat mixture. Sprinkle with sesame seeds, cover with the other top halves of the rolls, and serve immediately. For the full effect, enjoy this sandwich while the meat is nice and hot.

WAGYU BURGER
和牛バーガー

Look, we couldn't just give you one wagyu recipe and call it a day. Here's another masterpiece we cook with American Wagyu, this time ground for burgers. The secret here? Flaky panko breadcrumbs. Mixed into the wagyu, they keep your burger ultra moist and delicious. You end up with a charred, caramelized surface and super juicy interior. Burger heaven, baby!

SERVES 4

- 1 pound ground American Wagyu beef
- ¼ cup panko breadcrumbs
- 1 garlic clove, finely chopped
- 1 teaspoon salt
- ½ teaspoon freshly ground black pepper
- 1 tablespoon vegetable oil
- 1 tablespoon sake
- ¼ cup Demi-Glace Sauce (page 192)
- 4 Boston lettuce leaves (or other tender lettuce)
- 4 thin slices tomato (not too thick)
- 4 pretzel rolls or brioche buns, split and toasted
- ¼ red onion, thinly sliced
- 1 avocado, thinly sliced (optional)

In a large bowl, combine the wagyu, breadcrumbs, garlic, salt, and pepper. Using your hands, mix and squeeze the meat mixture together for about 2 minutes—this is important to get the right texture. You want to work the mixture until it becomes slightly sticky and starts to bind together. Using your hands helps you feel when the texture is right. (Wear food-prep gloves if you're feeling squeamish about this step.)

Divide the mixture into four equal portions and gently form into patties about ½ inch thick.

Heat the oil in a large skillet over medium heat. When the oil is hot but not smoking, add the patties and cook for 2 minutes on each side. After flipping the burgers, add the sake to the pan—it will sizzle and help release any browned bits from the bottom. Let the sake simmer for about 30 seconds, then pour in the demi-glace sauce. Reduce the heat to low and let the sauce simmer for about 1 minute, until it starts to thicken slightly. Use a spoon to baste the burgers with the sauce as they finish cooking.

For medium doneness, cook for another minute on each side after adding the sauce, flipping once more to evenly coat. The wagyu will shrink less than regular beef thanks to the panko, but it will still pull in a bit as it cooks. The burgers are done when they're nicely browned on the outside but still juicy within.

To assemble, place a lettuce leaf and a tomato slice on the bottom half of each toasted bun. Top with a burger patty and spoon the reduced sauce over it. Add some red onion slices and, if desired, avocado. Cover with the top bun and serve immediately.

P.S. Instead of the Demi-Glace Sauce you can use just ketchup, or better, equal parts ketchup and tonkatsu sauce (see page 236, or use Bulldog brand) for extra oomph!

KATSU SANDO

(PORK CUTLET SANDWICH)

トンカツサンド

In the pantheon of Japanese sandwiches, katsu sando reigns supreme. Found everywhere from 7-Elevens to five-star restaurants, it was invented in the 1930s by an *okami-san* (literally "female commander") who ran her and her chef husband's tonkatsu shop in Tokyo—a business pairing that endures in restaurants in Japan to this day—as a way to nourish the local geishas without risking a smudge on their kimonos. Thoughtful! She was likely inspired by the adoption of Western food influences at the time, including the humble toast, which began nudging rice off the traditional breakfast menu after it was introduced to Japan in the late nineteenth century. In Japan the bread of choice is *shokupan*, a.k.a. milk bread, a fluffier, lighter loaf than our typical white bread, with a slightly sweet taste and milky aroma, hence the name. You can find it in Japanese markets, or use your favorite sandwich bread.

SERVES 4

8 slices Japanese milk bread or other sandwich bread (in Japan they trim the crusts, up to you)

1 cup tonkatsu sauce (see page 236)

4 pork loin tonkatsu cutlets, freshly deep-fried (see page 236)

1 cup thinly sliced white cabbage (see Note, page 106)

Toast the bread and set aside.

To assemble a sandwich, slather 1 tablespoon of the tonkatsu sauce on a slice of bread and lay a piping hot tonkatsu cutlet on it. (Slather more sauce on the tonkatsu if you like it sloppy.) Top with a handful of sliced cabbage and cover with another piece of bread. To serve, you have two options: Trim the crusts and cut into quarters, like they do in Japan, to make it easier to eat; or slice your sandwich in half without trimming, like we do here. Your call.

Repeat with the remaining ingredients and serve the sandwiches immediately.

ALL HAIL THE SANDO!

Sandwiches gained popularity beginning in the late nineteenth century as Japanese people embraced all things Western, and were first served in *yoshoku* restaurants (which specialized in Western cooking). Fast forward to today and they've become a fixture of konbini (see page 103), *ekiben* (train station bento boxes), and every kid's lunchbox.

So what makes a sando a sando and not just any old sandwich? It starts with the traditional pillowy foundation: Japan's fluffy, milk-based white bread, *shokupan,* baked with a high moisture content and tight crumb that can stand up to sogginess. Then comes the signature Japanese fillings: pork katsu, lucious wagyu, deep-fried chicken, and rolled omelets—all fantastic! Finally, removing the crusts from the bread is de rigueur.

While shokupan rules the sando world, today Japanese cooks are expanding their bready choices, opting for rolls, pretzel buns, baguettes, and more. (And if you can't find shokupan, sub with a good white bread.) But no matter what wraps the sando, it's gotta nestle those mouthwatering Japanese ingredients inside!

RUNNY EGG KATSUDON

トロトロ玉子カツ丼

There are several competing origin stories about this dish. The one we love the best—which is likely apocryphal, but, hey, it's a great yarn!—traces katsudon to a hole-in-the-wall restaurant next to a major Tokyo university in the early twentieth century. There, a resourceful chef had a eureka moment when he decided to repurpose leftover tonkatsu, breaded pork cutlets, by simmering them with eggs and onions in a savory-sweet sauce and then pouring this beautiful mixture over steaming rice. According to legend, the dish quickly became a go-to-staple among students, first, because (obviously) it's so incredibly delicious, and second, because *katsu* means both "cutlet" and "to win" in Japanese, so the dish instantly established itself as the culinary equivalent of a rabbit's foot, especially around exam time—an eating tradition that luckily continues to this day. We came across the following version at another hole-in-the-wall, this one located in Tokyo's off-the-beaten-track Monzen Nakacho neighborhood (go visit, great food!) and loved it so much we had to share it with you. Here, an incredibly juicy, flavorful slab of pork loin tonkatsu is sliced and layered over a runny egg omelet, which itself is then layered over steaming rice before the whole thing is drizzled with savory-sweet homemade sauce. The tonkatsu doesn't get soggy, the crust stays perfectly crispy, the barely set egg is velvety and rich, and every bite is an incredible flavor revelation.

SERVES 4

TONKATSU SAUCE

1 cup Worcestershire sauce

¼ cup ketchup

¼ cup soy sauce

¼ cup mirin

TONKATSU

4 (4- to 5-ounce) pork loin cutlets

Salt and ground white pepper

½ cup all-purpose flour

2 eggs, beaten

2 cups panko breadcrumbs

4 cups vegetable oil, for frying

OMELETS

4 tablespoons vegetable oil

8 large eggs

Salt and ground white pepper

4 teaspoons karashi mustard, wasabi, or yuzu kosho (optional)

6 cups cooked rice, hot, for serving

Prepare the tonkatsu sauce. In a small saucepan, combine the Worcestershire sauce, ketchup, soy sauce, and mirin and bring to a boil over medium heat. Remove from the heat and set aside. (Note that this homemade tonkatsu sauce is thinner than the typical store-bought variety; this is a more updated version of the classic.)

Lay the pork loin pieces flat on a cutting board. With the back of your knife's blade, pound the surface of the meat to create ridges on both sides, about ¼ inch apart. This will help tenderize the pork. Next, make small cuts into the white fat around the edges to prevent curling during frying. Season both sides with salt and white pepper.

Set up a breading station: one shallow dish with the flour, one with the beaten eggs, and one with the breadcrumbs. Dredge each piece of pork in flour, shaking off the excess, then dip in the eggs, and finally coat thoroughly with panko, pressing gently to adhere. Make sure to cover all sides of the pork with the breadcrumbs. Set aside.

Prepare a deep-fry station. (Important: Read our note on deep-frying first, see page 213.) Fill a large cast-iron skillet (ideal) with at least 1½ inches of oil, enough so that the pork will float when it cooks. Attach a deep-fry or candy thermometer to the side of the skillet and heat the oil to 340°F over medium heat. It's crucial to use a thermometer to maintain the correct temperature throughout the frying process. On a work surface near the burner, prepare a paper towel–lined plate to drain the cooked pork.

Carefully add the pork to the hot oil, working in batches to avoid overcrowding (use at most half of the surface area of the oil to cook). Adjust the heat throughout the cooking time to maintain the temperature at about 340°F. Cook the pork for 5 to 6 minutes, depending on the thickness of the loin, flipping once halfway through, until the pork is golden brown and crispy. Transfer the pork to the prepared plate. If you can, stack the pieces standing up, like you're assembling a campfire; it will help drain the oil. When the pork is cool to the touch, slice each loin and set aside.

Prepare four serving bowls and add 1½ cups hot rice to each.

For the runny egg omelets, cook each one individually: Heat 1 tablespoon vegetable oil in a large nonstick skillet over medium-low heat. (Nonstick is ideal but cast-iron or stainless steel can work, too, just be careful not to preheat them for too long.) In a small bowl, gently beat 2 eggs to just combine, and season very lightly with salt and white pepper. When the skillet is heated, add the eggs and swirl in a circular motion for 10 to 15 seconds until the bottom just sets and the top is still very runny. Slide the omelet over a bowl of rice and repeat with the remaining eggs.

To assemble, in each bowl, drizzle 1 tablespoon tonkatsu sauce over the omelet. Arrange a portion of the sliced pork loin over the omelet and drizzle one more tablespoon tonkatsu sauce over. Garnish with karashi mustard, wasabi, or yuzu kosho if you'd like (pick one), and serve immediately. Encourage everyone to mix everything together for the full flavor experience.

BUTA KAKUNI

(BRAISED PORK BELLY)

豚角煮

Move over bacon. Who knew pork belly could be this good? *Kakuni,* which means "simmered squares" (of pork), is a Chinese import that arrived in Japan over a thousand years ago. The dish was originally a local specialty of Nagasaki, a key port city in the south that's been trading with China for centuries. Now popular across Japan, kakuni evolved into a symbol of prosperity and good fortune, and is often served for New Year's and other special occasions. But you don't need to wait for a milestone moment for the good fortune of enjoying this dish. Cook it now! What makes kakuni so special is that the pork is cooked twice: first, as a whole piece to break down and tenderize the meat, as well as keep its shape. And second, as square slices to absorb mouthwatering Japanese sweet-savory flavors and create a melt-in-your mouth, luscious texture. While Nagasaki citizens to this day demand kakuni to be kaku-kaku (perfectly square), don't sweat it if yours looks more like a rectangle. (It's okay, ours does, too.) Kakuni is one of those dishes that tastes even better the next day, so make sure to save some pieces, submerged in the cooling liquid, to reheat the next day or the day after. Finally, kakuni is amazing on ramen, so save some for noodles, too. Hmm . . . sounds like you should be making a double recipe. We won't argue with that.

SERVES 4

1 pound fresh pork belly, preferably with skin, in one rectangular piece, approximately 2 by 2 by 10 inches

1-inch piece ginger, unpeeled and roughly sliced

2 scallions, roughly chopped

½ cup sake

¼ cup soy sauce

3 tablespoons sugar

4 eggs

Karashi mustard (optional)

Place the pork belly in a pot that can fit it snugly. Add the ginger, scallions, and enough water to just cover the pork. Bring to a boil over high heat, then reduce to a low simmer. Cover the pot and let it cook gently for 1 hour. During this time, skim off any scum that rises to the surface.

Remove the pork from the pot and let it cool until you can handle it. Reserve 2 cups of the cooking liquid. Discard the rest and clean the pot. Once cooled, cut the pork into ¾-inch-thick pieces. Return the pork to the clean pot and add sake, soy sauce, sugar, and enough of the reserved cooking liquid to submerge the pork. Bring to a boil, then reduce to a gentle simmer.

CONTINUED →

BUTA KAKUNI, CONTINUED

Create an otoshibuta (drop lid, see page 210). Place the otoshibuta on top of the ingredients. You'll notice steam escaping (if the otoshibuta is bouncing around, lower the heat). Cook undisturbed for 30 minutes. The kakuni will start to give off an intoxicating, sweet-savory aroma at this point.

While the pork is simmering, prepare the soft-boiled eggs as follows: Fill a small saucepan and bring it to a boil over medium-high heat. Carefully add the eggs and cook for exactly 7 minutes. Transfer the saucepan to the sink. Pour out the boiling water and fill with cold running water to stop the cooking. As soon as the eggs are cool enough to touch, peel them and set aside.

Remove the otoshibuta and increase the heat to medium. Continue cooking for another 15 minutes, turning the pork once halfway through. The cooking liquid will reduce and become glossy, coating the pork with a beautiful glaze. The pork will be super tender and will easily break apart with chopsticks.

Add the eggs to the pot for the last 5 minutes of cooking, to allow them to absorb some of the flavorful braising liquid.

Serve in shallow bowls with some of the glossy sauce and a soft-boiled egg nestled alongside the pork. Add a dab of karashi mustard to the side of the bowl, if you like.

PORK TENDERLOIN WITH SPICY MISO

豚ヒレ辛味噌焼き

Here's a crowd-pleaser you can (and should) knock out for a quick weeknight dinner. This contemporary recipe centers on tenderloin, a lean, mild cut of pork that, as advertised, is exceptionally tender. It builds on traditional Japanese cooking techniques involving pork and miso. Fantastic Tonjiru (page 52) in our soup section is one example, and thin-sliced pork sautéed with miso, a popular home-cooking dish, is another. This dish evolves the latter by incorporating Western methods and ingredients—hello, butter and flour—with classic Japanese seasonings and aromatics. But why the pork and miso slow jam? Miso's rich umami flavor stands up to pork—arguably more popular in Japan than beef—and enhances the meat's natural flavors. Not only that, miso's enzymes penetrate the pork and make it even more tender. This pork is fast and easy to cook. Just add bowls of steaming white rice and maybe a salad (see page 105) alongside it, and you're set for din din.

SERVES 4

SAUCE

3 tablespoons sake

2 tablespoons aka miso

1 tablespoon mirin

2 teaspoons tobanjan

1 pound pork tenderloin, cut into 8 (½-inch-thick) medallions

Salt and ground white pepper

¼ cup all-purpose flour

1 tablespoon butter

1 tablespoon finely chopped garlic

1 teaspoon finely chopped ginger

FOR SERVING

1 tablespoon finely chopped scallions

Shredded cabbage (optional)

Make the sauce. In a small bowl, whisk together the sake, miso, mirin, and tobanjan until the miso is fully incorporated. Set aside.

Lay the pork medallions flat on a cutting board. Using the flat side of a chef's knife, gently pound each piece to flatten slightly. This helps tenderize the meat and creates more surface area for the sauce. Season the medallions with salt and white pepper on both sides.

Spread the flour on a plate and dredge the seasoned pork pieces, shaking off any excess. The flour will create a subtle crust that allows the sauce to adhere to the meat.

Heat a large skillet over medium heat. Add the butter and heat until it just starts to brown, about 30 seconds. Add the pork medallions and cook for 2 minutes on each side until nicely browned and just cooked through. Transfer the pork to a plate.

CONTINUED →

PORK TENDERLOIN WITH SPICY MISO, CONTINUED

In the same pan, add the garlic and ginger and cook, stirring constantly, until fragrant, about 30 seconds. Pour in the miso sauce and cook, stirring frequently, for 1 to 2 minutes, until the sauce begins to thicken and become glossy. Turn off the heat. (If the sauce becomes too thick, you can thin it with a small amount of water.)

Slice the pork and divide among four plates. Pour the sauce over the pork, making sure each medallion is well coated. Garnish with the scallions and cabbage, if desired, and serve immediately. (The cabbage adds a fresh, crunchy contrast.)

LAMB STEAK WITH GREEN YUZU KOSHO

羊ステーキ緑柚子胡椒焼き

In 1857, ten sheep were brought to Japan, and they moved into a magistrate's office on the far northern island of Hokkaido (the people working there must have loved that!), an area that basically served as the country's agricultural laboratory at the time (see page 48). Those first ten sheep exploded into over a million by the first quarter of the twentieth century. Despite the impressive numbers of sheep baa-ing across Hokkaido, it took decades for people in Japan to learn to love lamb, which only started to take off in the 1950s. Ever since, lamb is still associated with Hokkaido regional eats. Here we use lamb shoulder, a nicely marbled cut that's tender, juicy, and incredibly flavorful. Yuzu kosho, one of our favorite ingredients, offers bright, citrusy heat, a perfect counterpoint to the lamb.

SERVES 4

4 (6-ounce) lamb shoulder steaks

Salt and freshly ground black pepper

1 tablespoon olive oil

1 tablespoon butter

1 teaspoon finely chopped garlic

2 tablespoons sake

1 tablespoon mirin

1 tablespoon soy sauce

2 teaspoons green yuzu kosho

1 tablespoon chopped shiso leaves (optional)

Generously season both sides of the lamb steaks with salt and pepper. Heat a large skillet over medium-high heat. Add the olive oil and butter. When the butter has melted and starts to foam, add the lamb steaks.

Cook the lamb for about 3 minutes on each side for medium-rare, or adjust the time to your preferred doneness. Transfer the lamb to a plate and tent with foil to keep warm.

Reduce the heat to medium and add the garlic to the skillet. Cook, tilting the skillet so the garlic cooks in the fat, for about 30 seconds, until fragrant but not burnt. Add the sake, mirin, and soy sauce and stir to combine, scraping up any browned bits from the bottom of the pan.

Let the sauce simmer for about a minute, then stir in the yuzu kosho. Return the lamb and any accumulated juices to the skillet and cook for another minute, turning the lamb to coat it in the sauce.

Divide the lamb among four serving plates and spoon the sauce over the meat. Garnish with the shiso (if using). Serve immediately with forks and steak knives instead of chopsticks, as they do with this dish in Japan.

LAMB GYOZA

羊餃子

Tadashi first tasted this gyoza at a joint in Tokyo's Shitamachi neighborhood (see page 181) that specializes in a style of cooking hailing from Xi'an, China—the land of lamb in that country's far west. Unforgettable to Tadashi was the marriage of regional Chinese cooking with the addition of cumin and cilantro, and Japanese technique. While classic gyoza dipping sauce is a combination of rice vinegar, soy sauce, and rayu chili oil (1:1 vinegar to soy sauce, and rayu to taste), here we introduce one conjured from rice vinegar, salt, and white pepper, which has become trendy these days for all gyoza styles (and you know we're SO on trend). Try both! A note about gyoza skins: Many brands are ultra-processed and loaded with junk ingredients, which is not cool in our book. Look for Japanese gyoza skins in the frozen section of Asian markets, which tend to stick to the basic ingredients (always read the label). Alternatively, for you adventurous souls out there, we include a method for making homemade gyoza skins (see page 201), which actually are pretty easy to knock out, but take a little time.

MAKES ABOUT 24 GYOZA

Potato starch (katakuriko) for dusting, plus 1 tablespoon for the "glue"

2 cups finely chopped green cabbage (you can do this with a food processor)

1 teaspoon salt

½ pound ground lamb (see Note)

½ cup finely chopped onion

2 teaspoons finely chopped garlic

½ teaspoon ground cumin

½ teaspoon ground white pepper

2 teaspoons soy sauce

½ cup chopped cilantro

3 tablespoons warm water

24 gyoza skins (store-bought or homemade, see page 201)

1 tablespoon plus 1 teaspoon vegetable oil (we like avocado oil)

⅔ cup water, for steaming

DIPPING SAUCE

2 tablespoons rice vinegar

½ teaspoon salt

¼ teaspoon ground white pepper

Dust a baking sheet with potato starch for the finished gyoza and have a clean, dry kitchen towel ready to cover them. Set aside.

In a large bowl, combine the cabbage and salt. Mix well with your hands, really massaging the salt into the cabbage until it starts to soften and release liquid. Let sit for 10 minutes. Transfer the cabbage to a clean kitchen towel, gather the corners together, and twist tightly over the sink, squeezing out as much liquid as possible. Keep twisting and squeezing until no more water drips out. This step is crucial for preventing soggy gyoza.

In a large bowl, combine the squeezed cabbage, ground lamb, onion, garlic, cumin, white pepper, soy sauce, and cilantro. Using your hands again, mix and squeeze the ingredients together vigorously for about 2 minutes. You want to work the mixture until it becomes sticky and holds together when pressed. It should start to feel almost paste-like but still have distinct pieces of cabbage visible. The texture should be cohesive enough that when you pick up a small amount, it holds together in a clump.

CONTINUED →

LAMB GYOZA, CONTINUED

In a small bowl, combine 1 tablespoon potato starch with 3 tablespoons warm water. This is the "glue" for sealing the gyoza.

To fold the gyoza, hold a skin in the palm of one hand with the floured-side down. Moisten the entire edge with the starch mixture. Place about 1 tablespoon of filling in the center of the skin, then fold the skin so the edges touch. Now use the index fingers and thumbs of both hands to fold the skin and pinch it together to create 5 or 6 pleats, pressing each pleat firmly against the flat back layer to seal. The pleats should all face the same direction, creating a gentle curve in the dumpling. Place the finished gyoza on the prepared sheet, pleated-side up, and cover with the kitchen towel while you make the rest.

Heat a large skillet (we use cast iron with a lid) over medium heat. Add 1 tablespoon of the oil and swirl to coat the bottom. Arrange the gyoza in a single layer, flat-side down (it's okay if they're touching). Cook uncovered for 1 to 2 minutes, until the bottoms start to turn golden brown.

Carefully pour ⅔ cup water around the edges of the pan; it will sizzle and steam vigorously. Immediately cover the skillet with a lid and steam for 5 minutes. Remove the lid and continue cooking until the water evaporates completely, about 2 minutes more. Add the remaining 1 teaspoon oil around the edges and cook for 1 minute more, until the bottoms are crispy and golden brown.

While the gyoza cooks, prepare the dipping sauce. In a small bowl, combine the rice vinegar, salt, and white pepper.

Transfer the finished gyoza to a serving plate, crispy-side up, and serve immediately with the dipping sauce alongside.

P.S. You can freeze uncooked gyoza. Arrange them on a parchment-lined baking sheet and freeze until solid, then transfer to a freezer bag. Store for up to a month. Cook them straight from frozen; just add an extra minute to the steaming time.

NOTE

If you can't find ground lamb in your local market, you can buy lamb shoulder and use a food processor to create the same result. You want the lamb to be roughly ground rather than finely chopped.

GYOZA LOVE

These crescent-shaped-and-pleated dumplings originated in China, like their dumpling cousins, shumai (see page 172). Brought back by Japanese soldiers returning from China after World War II, they rapidly became a staple dish because, well, they tasted so damn good. Unlike the original *jiaozi*, the Japanese version is typically loaded with garlic and garlic chives, and they're usually cooked in the uniquely yaki-gyoza style, where the dumplings are both fried and steamed in the same pan, resulting in crispy toasted skin on one side and beautifully tender skin on the other. The steaming yields another benefit, too, transforming the filling into juicy, aromatic, flavorful, heavenly bites (need we say more?). And besides their irresistible, mouthwatering appeal, their iconic crescent shape is an ancient Chinese symbol of wealth and good fortune, so a nice two-fer as these guys are heading down the hatch. The standard-bearer gyoza is pork and green cabbage-based (see our book *Japanese Soul Cooking* for the recipe) and is traditionally served with a dipping sauce. In this book we introduce two other styles we absolutely love: lamb (see page 245) and chicken (see page 197). Finally, keep this in mind—the folding technique takes a little practice. But don't be intimidated, and keep at it. Remember, your gyoza will still taste amazing even if they're not perfectly folded. Practice, practice, practice.

GLOSSARY

ABURA AGE Thin tofu pouches that are deep-fried until golden and puffy with hollow centers.

AKA MISO Reddish-brown miso with a robust flavor and rich umami, aged one to three years; pairs well with hearty ingredients.

AONORI Powdered dried green seaweed with an intense oceanic flavor and a vibrant emerald color.

AWASE The practice of blending different varieties of miso to create complex, nuanced flavors.

BUBU ARARE Tiny bubble-shaped rice crackers that add a playful crunch and contrast.

DAIKON OROSHI Finely grated daikon radish that aids digestion and cuts through rich foods while adding fresh flavor.

DONKO SHIITAKE Premium dried shiitake mushrooms with thick caps and intensely concentrated flavor.

GENMAI Brown rice with bran and germ intact; nutty flavor and higher nutritional value than white rice.

HAIGA MAI Rice with bran removed but nutritious germ intact; best of both worlds.

HARI SHOGA Ginger cut into fine needle-like strips; adds zesty brightness and visual appeal to dishes.

HATCHO MISO Chocolate-colored miso from Aichi Prefecture, aged two to three years using just soybeans and salt; intense flavor and powerful umami.

HIJIKI Black seaweed with pronounced mineral flavor, harvested from rocky coastlines for millennia; reconstitute before cooking.

HOSHI SHIITAKE Dried shiitake mushrooms with concentrated umami intensity; rehydrate to unlock their powerful flavor.

IRI SAKE The process of heating sake to evaporate alcohol while preserving flavor.

JIDORI Heritage chicken breeds raised to exacting standards; prized for exceptional flavor and texture.

KARASHI Fiery Japanese mustard with sinus-clearing heat; traditional condiment for fried foods.

KATAKURIKO Fine potato starch used for coating; creates delicate, crispy exteriors without absorbing excess oil when frying.

KATSUOBUSHI Skipjack tuna that has been dried, fermented, smoked, and shaved into flakes; foundational umami powerhouse essential for traditional dashi.

KINUGOSHI Silken tofu with a delicate, custard-like texture; made without pressing.

KISHIMEN Flat, wide noodles from Nagoya; distinctive shape allows sauce to cling perfectly to its broad surface.

KIZAMI NORI Finely shredded nori seaweed used as garnish or flavor enhancement.

KOJI Rice mold used for fermentation; Japan's "national mold," enabling flavor transformations.

KOMBU Mineral-rich edible kelp with highest natural concentration of glutamate; essential dashi ingredient.

ME HIJIKI Tender leaf section of hijiki seaweed; softer texture than stem sections.

MIRIN Sweet cooking seasoning with complex flavor; adds luster, umami, and subtle sweetness.

MISO Fermented soybean paste with complex umami flavor; Japan's culinary cornerstone.

NAGAHIJIKI "Long hijiki" seaweed stem with robust, chewy texture and earthy flavor; reconstitute before using.

NERI GOMA Japanese sesame paste made from toasted sesame seeds; nuttier and more aromatic than tahini.

OTOSHIBUTA Traditional drop lid smaller than cooking pot; ensures gentle, even simmering and prevents ingredients from breaking apart.

RANGIRI Diagonal cutting technique that creates irregular surfaces to absorb flavors better.

RAYU Chile-infused sesame oil with deep, warming heat; essential condiment for gyoza.

RENKON Lotus root, recognizable for its distinctive hole pattern; maintains crisp, crunchy texture when cooked.

SAKE KASU Leftover lees from sake brewing; flavorful by-product used in cooking.

SANSHO Japanese pepper with a citrusy, numbing quality; uniquely aromatic and mouth-tingling.

SATOIMO Taro root; nutty flavor; creamy yet slightly slimy texture when cooked.

SHAMOJI Rice paddle used for mixing and serving rice without damaging grains.

SHIBORI "Wrung out" preparation technique for sliced scallions; removes excess moisture and bitterness for concentrated flavor.

SHICHIMI TOGARASHI Seven-spice chile pepper mixture with complex heat profile; customizable blend.

SHIITAKE Umami-rich mushroom variety with distinctive aroma; essential in Japanese cuisine.

SHIMEJI Delicate mushroom clusters with mild flavor when raw; develops nutty taste when cooked.

SHIOKOJI Salt combined with koji mold; functions as a natural meat tenderizer and flavor enhancer with ancient roots in preservation.

SHIRO MISO Straw-colored "white" miso with milder flavor profile; typically aged three to six months; versatile for everyday use.

SHISO Aromatic herb with a minty-basil flavor; found in both green and purple varieties.

SHOKUPAN Japanese milk bread with cloud-like texture; a sandwich essential in Japan.

TOBANJAN Spicy fermented bean paste that adds complex heat and depth to dishes.

UMEBOSHI Pickled plum with intense sour-salty flavor and distinctive ruby color; traditional rice ball filling.

USUKUCHI Light-colored soy sauce with saltier, more delicate flavor than regular shoyu; preserves ingredients' natural colors.

WAGYU Japanese beef with exceptional marbling; livestock breed raised with meticulous care.

WAKAME Tender seaweed with mild flavor and silky texture; commonly used in soups and salads, reconstitute before using.

WASABI Fresh, herbaceous condiment grated from the wasabi rhizome; produces a clean heat that dissipates quickly.

YUZU KOSHO Fermented paste of yuzu citrus zest and chiles; versatile condiment that provides bright, aromatic heat.

ACKNOWLEDGMENTS

We would like to thank Harris's life partner, the author and yoga baddie Susanna Harwood Rubin, for reading the manuscript and sharing her deft editorial comments; our longtime literary agent and champion, the inimitable Angela Miller; our supremely talented photographer, Janice Chung, whose work in *The New York Times* first blew us away and who was such an absolute delight to collaborate and travel with; our stylist, Gowun Lee; the outstanding editorial and creative team at Ten Speed Press; all our wonderful and dedicated recipe testers across the USA; our friend, travel buddy, and erstwhile dishwasher, Sasha "Sasha san" Varlamov (side gig when he's not launching tech startups); our Tokyo pals, the amazing Mirei Yamagata and her sister Ema; our friend Yuko Suzuki in Osaka; all the incredible folks in Japan who extended so much warmth and kindness to us including: Yoshiteru Ikegawa of Torikishi, Tokyo; Hideyuki Asa of Torigin, Ginza; Chihiro Hagiwara of Nanca, Tokyo; Yoshie and Yosuke Yoguchi of Yaguya, Tokyo; Yosuke Sumiya of Mikawa Mirin; Yoshiyuki Aoki of Minamigura Tamari shoyu; Kaoru Sawada of the Sawada sake brewery; the eminent Shintaro Asai of Maruya Hatcho Miso; wagyu rancher and University of Nebraska alum Muneharu Ozaki in Miyazaki (go Cornhuskers!); Yasunari Yamashina of the Yamashina Tea Company in Kyushu; Munehiro Sata of Ayayane brewery in Kagoshima; and Sean MacPherson of the Chelsea Hotel, New York.

iNDEX

TEN SPEED PRESS
An imprint of the Crown Publishing Group
A division of Penguin Random House LLC
1745 Broadway
New York, NY 10019
tenspeed.com
penguinrandomhouse.com

Typefaces: Studio Aurora's Quipo, Colophon Foundry's Apercu, Monotype's Shorai Sans

Library of Congress Cataloging-in-Publication Data has been applied for.

Hardcover ISBN 978-0-593-83701-6
Ebook ISBN 978-0-593-83702-3

Acquiring editor: Claire Yee | Project editor: Dena Rayess
Production editor: Terry Deal
Designer: Annie Marino | Art director: Emma Campion
Production designer: Mari Gill
Production and prepress color manager: Jane Chinn
Food stylist: Gowun Lee
Compositor: Faith Hague
Copy editor: Eldes Tran | Proofreaders: Jonathan Milder, Tess Rossi | Indexer: Ina Gravitz
Publicist: David Hawk | Marketer: Stephanie Davis

Manufactured in China

10 9 8 7 6 5 4 3 2 1

First Edition

The authorized representative in the EU for product safety and compliance is Penguin Random House Ireland, Morrison Chambers, 32 Nassau Street, Dublin D02 YH68, Ireland, https://eu-contact.penguin.ie.

楽々日本料理